# The Tender Scar

## Scar

### Life After the Death of a Spouse

SECOND EDITION

## Richard L. Mabry

Kregel
*Publications*

*The Tender Scar: Life After the Death of a Spouse*
© 2006, 2017 by Richard L. Mabry
Second edition 2017

Published by Kregel Publications, a division of Kregel, Inc., 2450 Oak Industrial Dr. NE, Grand Rapids, MI 49505.

The authors and publisher are not engaged in rendering medical or psychological services, and this book is not intended as a guide to diagnose or treat medical or psychological problems. If medical, psychological, or other expert assistance is required, the reader should seek the services of a healthcare provider or certified counselor.

ISBN 978-0-8254-4476-0

Printed in the United States of America
17 18 19 20 21 22 23 24 25 / 5 4 3 2 1

# Contents

# Preface to the
# Second Edition

When I first tried to write *The Tender Scar* I was tempted to portray myself in a better light by explaining and justifying some of my actions and attitudes. It didn't work. It was only when I succeeded in transferring my unedited feelings to paper, opening myself to criticism and making myself vulnerable, that the book became the kind of work I wanted it to be. The book carries with it some of the raw emotions I felt, and perhaps that's why it's helped so many others.

*The Tender Scar* has been ministering for a decade to those touched by the loss of a spouse. When the publishers asked me about a revision, my reply was, "This book was written while the pain of Cynthia's death was still fresh enough to make my thoughts valid. I don't want to change a thing."

More than a year after Cynthia's death, God blessed me once more with the love of a wonderful and understanding woman, Kay. I find her insights into the writing life I've slipped into after my retirement from medicine both accurate and helpful, although sometimes they sting a bit. It was Kay who suggested that I might add a chapter to the book about what I've now experienced for more than fifteen years—a second marriage that creates a blended family. And as my new journey with Kay differs from my journey with Cynthia, you'll find my writing in this new chapter to differ from my writing in the first edition of *The Tender Scar*.

I hope you find the totality of this work helpful.

# Preface to the First Edition

If you've picked up this book, chances are that you—or someone dear to you—have lost a loved one. Perhaps a spouse.

Every marriage includes the dream of "living happily ever after." Some part of us realizes, of course, that the time we share together with our spouses will eventually end. But the human tendency is to put that bit of reality aside. Too often we successfully ignore it until our "ever after" comes to a screeching halt. Mine did at 7:30 p.m. on Tuesday, September 14, 1999. This book stems from the aftermath of that event and is based on my observations and comments as someone who's been there, done that, survived, and continues to work at reaching the other side of grief. It is unapologetically personal, because my experience is all I can write about with certainty. It has a Christian perspective, because both Cynthia and I made Christ an integral part of our lives and our marriage. And although "happily ever after" might not be possible, may these pages offer comfort and inspiration that starts you on the road to "hopefully ever after."

One bit of advice I received after Cynthia's death was to begin journaling. This can be a means of achieving some catharsis of the pent-up and varied emotions experienced by the recently bereaved. My journaling began as emails to my family, my closest friends, and my pastor, along with an occasional letter written posthumously to Cynthia as well as entries meant just for me. This book is an outgrowth of that journaling. I have taken the seminal portions (the text in *italics* at the beginning of each chapter) and used them as jumping-off points for discussion, including recommendations and words of comfort for the bereaved. I've tried to convey the emotions I was feeling—the good and the bad, the highs and the lows—hoping that this will help you know that others have felt the same way you do. My comments offer help for the person wondering, "When will this end?" or "Is it normal to feel this way?" or "What have other people done about this?"

You may have already heard or read that healing from the death of a spouse will take about a year, two years at most. I've learned differently. The length of that journey has been indeterminate for me, as it will be for you. But I'm far enough along on the path to look back from a clearer perspective and comment on the emotions and reactions that are common to the grieving individual. If even one chapter of this book helps just one person get through his or her own passage through the valley of the shadow of death, then my efforts will have been worth it. Thank you for sharing my journey.

> We are pressed on every side by troubles, but we are not crushed.
> We are perplexed, but not driven to despair. (2 Cor. 4:8)

*Dear Lord, we acknowledge that Your ways are not our ways. Your agenda doesn't always coincide with ours. Only in the fullness of time, when we stand before Your throne, will we truly understand why terrible things happen in this world. We pray that those who mourn will be comforted, those who feel incomplete will achieve healing, and that, in all we do and say, we will have the grace to finally say with a willing heart, "Thy will be done." Grant this peace to all those experiencing the desolation of loss. We pray in Your healing name, amen.*

# ACKNOWLEDGMENTS

This book could never have become a reality without the help and inspiration of a number of people. I acknowledge the loving support given me by my church families at both Cliff Temple Baptist Church and Duncanville's First Baptist Church, and by my pastors, Glen Schmucker, Charles Lovell, and Keith Brister. I also received encouragement from my children and their spouses—Allen and Lynne, Brian and Catherine, and Ann. God has given me a second blessing in the form of a loving and caring wife, Kay, who has been not only wonderfully understanding and helpful during my continuing journey but has been my strong right arm during the process of creating this book. The experience of attending the Christian Writers Workshop in Glorieta, New Mexico, was a watershed event in my life and my Christian experience. From that point, God inspired me, and mentors helped me, to take an unformed conglomeration of journaling and transform it into the pages you see here.

I truly believe that, although we may not understand how or why, God can take terrible events and use them for eventual good. If this book helps you, it is just more evidence of His willingness to do just that and a demonstration of His power and His love for us.

# One

# PLAYING THE BLAME GAME

"Did I do everything I could?" One of the overwhelming emotions that affect the grieving individual is guilt. The games of "What if I had . . . ?" and "If only I could have . . ." or even "I should have . . ." are endless. When considered through the perspective of time, most of us see these speculations as useless.

> *I still continue to replay the three-plus hours between the time of Cynthia's stroke and the surgery meant to relieve the pressure in her brain. I repeatedly torture myself with thoughts of "Could we have gotten her to the medical center more quickly?" or "Should I have done this or that to speed up the process?" I'm a doctor, and I'm supposed to help people, to intervene, to take action. But things dragged on so slowly, and I felt so powerless. My colleagues tell me that Cynthia's stroke was not a survivable injury, and everything that could be done was done. But, despite its lack of logic, I've continued to grieve over my inability to make things happen faster and better. I wonder if I'll ever get over this guilt.* (Author's email to a friend who suffered a similar loss)

Husbands and wives spend years taking care of each other, thinking of their spouses' needs, often subjugating their own desires and plans for those of their mates. When a spouse dies, whether quickly or after an extended period of illness, the opportunity for what-if scenarios and the attendant guilt is enormous. These feelings can linger for months and years, crippling the surviving spouse with guilt. In most cases, an unbiased observer will tell us we did everything we could. But even if we didn't, we can't change the final outcome. As Omar Khayyam wrote, "The Moving Finger writes; and having writ, moves on."

There is also a feeling of guilt at being the one left alive. "Why couldn't it have been me?" we think. This may lead, in turn, to an attitude of "I shouldn't do anything for myself. I don't deserve to be happy." Often we can't enjoy the simple pleasures of life because we think our spouses will never again enjoy the things we continue to experience, and for that we blame ourselves. The little voice inside us says, "Why should I enjoy the sunrise when my spouse will never see another one?" The response may not be rational, but it certainly is real—and crippling.

Despite all the good advice in the world, guilt and what-ifs are part of grieving. The best advice I can offer is to talk things over with someone (repeatedly, if necessary), starting with an unbiased family member or friend. Expand the support base from there until you're able to not only say, "I did what I could at the time," but also, "I can't change it now."

Now may be the time to look for a support group. Sometimes you may find that friends, and even church staff, are too close to you. It's hard to open up around these people because you don't want to reveal your frailties and what you may perceive as shortcomings. If you're computer literate, you may find help through an online resource such as WidowNet (www.WidowNet.org), where it's possible to unburden yourself and receive advice and support in relative anonymity. In addition, though, it's best to seek human contact for face-to-face support. I was fortunate to find a widowed persons support group in my area through AARP.

Whatever the means chosen, now is the time to begin talking out the what-ifs and to start dealing with the survivor guilt that can plague the widowed for months and sometimes years. The feeling of guilt is normal, natural, and—to a degree—understandable. But it need not be permanent.

> Who can discern their own errors?
> Forgive my hidden faults.
>
> (Ps. 19:12 NIV)

*Loving Father, forgive us when we sometimes take responsibility for things we can't control. We are imperfect, faulted, and frail. Pardon us when we stumble, admonish us when we stray, but always keep us aware that You are a God of mercy, grace, and love. We accept that we cannot undo our actions, revise our omissions, or change what we've already done. But we acknowledge that in Your love we start each day forgiven and cleansed. Help us to move forward, not necessarily always understanding but always trusting. In Your name, amen.*

# CONFRONTING END-OF-LIFE ISSUES

A difficult decision in end-of-life situations is to remove life support. Physicians offer their best counsel, and family and friends provide support, but the decision leaves lingering doubt and guilt in the mind of the person charged with that ultimate responsibility.

*After Cynthia's massive stroke, the neurosurgeons said, "Let's give it some time." I think they believed she would soon die peacefully, because later they confided that they knew her episode was not a survivable one. For two weeks, she was on life support, and every day I looked for change but didn't see any. As a doctor, I knew she was already essentially dead, but as a husband I couldn't give up hope. Finally, the neurosurgeon said, "Do you want to wait for her to eventually die, or are you ready to withdraw life support?" Cynthia and I had talked this over long ago, we both had living wills, and in my heart I knew what she would want. We took her off the ventilator and she gently slipped away. I cried uncontrollably when I made that decision. I cried even more when Cynthia breathed her last, and I'm crying now as I write about it months later. Even with all that justification, since that time I have suffered terribly, wondering if she might have eventually recovered (I'm told she never would), wondering whether I acted in order to end her state of nonrecoverable vegetative existence or to put a stop to my personal hell on earth as I waited in the ICU for an awakening that was not going to come in this life.* (Author's email to an online contact who had taken her husband off life support)

In the past few decades, medical science has made gigantic strides, providing avenues to cure and control diseases and conditions that at one time were tantamount to a death sentence. As a result, the average life expectancy in our country continues to climb. But all this comes at a price. Each of us recognizes that in some situations life may be prolonged, but sometimes at costs that may include constant pain and debilitating side effects—not to mention the emotional and economic toll exacted by such measures. This is especially true for situations in which cancer and other malignancies have reached a stage at which there is no longer any hope for cure or even remission. All that can be hoped for is slowing the inevitable progression of the disease, allowing the afflicted person a bit more time to be with his or her family and friends. Eventually a point may be reached at which the patient is so dulled by ever-increasing amounts of pain medication, so debilitated by the disease, that the prospect of death offers the only hope of release.

When are heroic measures and intensive treatment no longer in anyone's best interest? The presence of a living will makes this decision easier, but not everyone has expended the time and effort to execute one. Whether or not a living will is in place, the spouse or responsible family member must first of all seek wise counsel from a physician. None of us can predict the future, and physicians are certainly no exception, but an experienced doctor can help immeasurably by guiding decisions at such a time.

In addition, sharing all the circumstances openly with other close members of the family will ease the burden of the one making the decision. There may be a single person (generally a spouse or the eldest child) on whom the responsibility falls for making the ulti-mate choice to discontinue treatment except for palliative measures aimed at comfort. But be sure to tell all family members about what is influencing your decision before—not after—it is made.

Finally, spiritual guidance is imperative. The Bible is essentially silent (or at best ambiguous) about end-of-life decisions, but the sup-port of clergy and church family can help and should be allowed and actively sought. And, of course, prayer is important—not just one-way prayer that asks for guidance, but also two-way prayer in which you pour out your anguish to God, and then, in worshipful silence, allow God to speak to you. Don't expect a rushing wind or a burning bush, but do anticipate a peace from letting God help you with your burden.

When a loved one suffers a stroke and lies comatose for a prolonged period of time, the natural reaction is to think, "She'll recover—all that's needed is time." Medical science, though inexact, can give some guidance. When all signs indicate that the person who lies silent (being maintained on a respirator and fed via a tube, or receiv-ing intravenous fluids) has no prospect of ever again being a sentient human, it should—at least theoretically—be easy to make the decision to remove life support. At this point we sometimes encounter a story (often passed on second- or third-hand) of a person who has been in a coma for months or years and suddenly recovers. Much as we'd like to think our loved one would do likewise, let me warn you: those cases—most often reported not in medical journals but in newspa-pers and magazines—represent highly unusual situations in which there was always a chance (however slim) of recovery. In most cases of massive stroke or extreme head injury, recovery is not even a pos-sibility. Skilled clinicians can generally assess the amount of perma-nent injury to the brain and realistically predict whether any degree of recovery is possible. Ask questions, get advice, and lean on it.

It is helpful when a husband and wife are able to frankly discuss all these matters before the fact. I was fortunate because Cynthia and I—long before I was called upon to make a decision—openly shared our feelings about prolonging nonproductive life. We had some warning, since we knew that she had a malformation of blood vessels in the brain. She considered all the possible scenarios, and then made her wishes clear. Whether or not I agreed with them, I had unambiguous marching orders when the time came to make the decision.

You may be asking, "Why all this discussion about how to handle the removal of life support? That's all past me now." There are two reasons. First, this chapter may spark you to make your own wishes evident to your family members, preferably in the form of a living will, but certainly at least in clear conversation. Many hospitals have living will forms and patient representatives who will help you execute one. And, in the shadow of your recent loss, right now may be the best time for you to consider this step.

The second reason is to provide counsel and comfort to you if you have already made this tough decision. There are many circumstances that can leave a life hanging on by the thread of artificial life support. When this occurs, decisions must be made, and they are never easy, but here are some guiding principles: take the best available medical counsel, talk it over with the closest family members, seek spiritual guidance, and then make the best decision you can make. When that's been done, try not to look back and second guess yourself after it's all over. You've done your best. That's all anyone can do.

> I can see now, GOD, that your decisions are right;
> your testing has taught me what's true and right.
> Oh, love me—and right now!—hold me tight!
> just the way you promised.
>
> (Ps. 119:75–76 MSG)

*Caring Father, sometimes we're called upon to make decisions that weigh upon us for months and years afterward. Teach us to do our very best and then to peacefully accept it's over and done, the results unchangeable. Help us to know that Your love for us never changes and Your decisions are never wrong. We put You in control, and thank You for the peace that doing so gives. In Your loving name, amen.*

# Three

# EXPERIENCING TEARS AND SHOCK

From early childhood, we're admonished not to cry. We're told to hold our emotions in check. But grief is accompanied by tears, anger, frustration, and a flood of other emotions. All of this is normal, but nonetheless frustrating.

*Well, I thought I could do it. It's been five days since Cynthia's death. I awoke this morning at 5 a.m. I spent the morning cleaning out her cosmetics (the unused ones will go to a battered women's shelter). I cried until I thought I couldn't cry any more. Finally, I had to get out of the house and away from all the things that remind me of Cynthia. It's Sunday, and I decided to slip unobtrusively into the church just after it started. I was able to sneak into the balcony without attracting attention, but I lasted about five minutes before I broke down, began crying, and had to leave. I can't describe all the emotions I'm feeling. I continue to alternately pray for strength and feel angry/hurt/confused with God for what has happened.*

*I try to think back and feel good about the past forty-plus years, and I do—but then I realize that my life will absolutely never be the same. I'm crying now as I write this, and for me that's absolutely out of character. I've always been the strong one, comforting and helping others. I'm not the same . . . and maybe I never will be again. Nothing has ever hit me as hard as this.* (Author's email to his pastor)

Although I'm told I acted rationally at the time, the two weeks when Cynthia lay in the ICU and the days following her death are a blur. Part of this relative amnesia is caused by the brain's blocking out extremely unpleasant memories. I do know I cried uncontrollably at times, at the slightest provocation. I was able to make decisions about final arrangements and other needful things. I even offered the prayer at the family meal before her memorial service, but I honestly don't remember much about all that. I was truly on autopilot.

The shock of the death of a close loved one can have both physical and emotional consequences. At these times, a bereaved spouse who has a heart condition or high blood pressure would do well to consult a physician. The stress of the event might place him or her in jeopardy of a heart attack or stroke. Both stimulants and depressants (such as alcohol) should be used with great care, if at all. And it may be wise to discuss with your physician, either now or at some time in the future, the possibility of a mild sleeping pill to allow for adequate rest.

In the weeks and months that follow, watch for the signs of depression: difficulty concentrating, trouble sleeping, lack of appetite, loss of energy, apathy, and thoughts of suicide. (For more details, see sites such as www.about-depression.com.) There is no disgrace in considering taking prescription antidepressants during this time. I resisted doing so for almost three months, finally giving in to the suggestions of my family and my physician. Their intervention led me to being dramatically helped. Although antidepressants have their own potential side effects (which your doctor and pharmacist will discuss with you) and do not provide instant relief, they can smooth out the roller-coaster of emotions experienced by a recently bereaved person.

Finally, be aware that what you're likely experiencing is a typical situational depression. That is, something very bad has happened in your life, something that would cause emotional distress for any normal person, and as a result you've begun to exhibit the signs and symptoms of clinical depression. It's a very normal reaction, and it is (or should be) a self-limited condition that will eventually clear. Some people have it to a greater degree than others, and sometimes help is needed in dealing with it. Just be thankful for the "better living through chemistry" that your physician can add, along with the counsel and support you will receive from those around you. Take comfort that, whether you are in the depths of depression or on the mountaintops of joy, God is with you. Lean on Him.

> Why are you in despair, O my soul? And why are you restless and disturbed within me? Hope in God and wait expectantly for Him, for I shall again praise Him, the help of my [sad] countenance and my God. (Ps. 43:5 AMP)

≈

*Ever-present Father, You have promised You will not leave us alone or comfortless. When we feel most bereft, help us to reach out to You. When we are angry with You, when we are hurt, and when we continue to wonder why, reach down and touch us so we can know that, even when we find it hard to love You, You love us. Give us the faith that looks beyond today and the courage to travel on. In Jesus's sustaining name, amen.*

# Four

# AVOIDING A SHRINE TO GRIEF

Disposing of personal possessions is, for the bereaved survivor, among the most difficult of tasks. The process not only triggers emotions but also creates the temptation to turn these possessions into a shrine for the deceased loved one.

*I felt as though I was making progress the past few days, but trying to clean out Cynthia's closet started it all over again. Getting rid of her clothes is yet another reminder that she is gone. Part of me keeps saying, "But if the clothes are gone, what will she wear when she comes back?" While Cynthia was in the ICU, I even saved newspapers, thinking, "She'll want to catch up on what happened while she was in a coma." It took me weeks to throw those papers away. Hope outstrips logic in these situations. It's as though everything I do that removes something of hers from our home takes her further and further away on a journey from which my head knows she won't return, while my heart keeps holding out futile hope.*

*I believe Cynthia would have already dealt with this if the situation were reversed. She was such a commonsense individual. I don't want to "build a shrine in the closet" to her, as some widowed persons seem to do. Rather than worshipping those articles of clothing, I know she would tell me that they need to go to someone who can get some good from them. Allen and Lynne* [my son and daughter-in-law] *have volunteered to go through the closets while I'm gone next week, carrying the clothes to their church's outreach ministry, and I've thanked them for the love and courage required to do this. I just can't do it. . . . I don't know that I ever could.* (Author's journal)

After the initial shock of loss has begun to subside, there comes a time when those left behind must deal with the physical possessions of the one who has died. This can be a daunting task, both from the standpoint of the emotional trauma involved and the time and effort required. And it comes at a period when grief and depression typically sap the energy of the survivor.

The simplest decisions take on magnified significance in these circumstances. Take the task of dealing with clothes. Some people find it difficult, even impossible, to part with these symbols of their lost loved ones. They like to finger the clothing, smell the perfume or aftershave fragrance that often clings to them, imagine the circumstances when they last saw the clothes being worn. If they give the clothes to a friend or relative, can they tolerate seeing them worn by another person? Will that sight trigger memories that will be painful and open wounds that have only just begun to heal? If the slightest possibility exists that this will be the case, it is best to give the clothing to a charitable organization such as a homeless shelter, a church's outreach ministry, a home for battered spouses, or some similar entity. Most cities present an opportunity for such a benevolent (and worthy) donation. If the physical act of clearing the closet is emotionally painful (as it almost always is), enlist the help of family members or friends.

Unopened cosmetics or toiletries, books that are not meaningful to the survivor, and other personal articles (golf clubs, for example) must be disposed of in some fashion. Don't hesitate to seek the advice and assistance of others in this task. Look for ways in which others can benefit from this disposition, and don't be afraid to say, "I need to wait a while before making a decision about this." This is especially true of jewelry, antiques, and other things that are most likely to be of both sentimental and/or monetary value. I strongly advise putting off the disposition of such things for several months, perhaps a year or more, when emotion plays less of a part in the decision-making process.

There's one question for which there is no one right or wrong answer: "What about the wedding rings?" Should the deceased be buried with his or her wedding ring on, or should the ring be saved for future generations? At what point does the survivor cease to wear his or her wedding ring? I chose to keep Cynthia's ring, hoping it would be meaningful to a child or grandchild. Your own wedding ring should be worn until you begin to feel right about taking it off. After years of wearing a ring, a bare finger feels strangely empty. When the wedding ring is finally removed, many people, myself included, choose to substitute another ring (often a gift from the spouse who has died) on the third finger of the left hand.

There are many ways in which the survivor is tempted to build a shrine to grief—by leaving the departed one's voice on the answering machine, by leaving a room exactly as the loved one left it, even by setting an extra place at the table at every meal. If our Christian faith teaches us anything, it is that the loss we feel is a temporary one, and that our loved ones have gone on to another life we will someday share. Until then, at whatever speed and in whatever way seems appropriate, we need to turn them loose, wish them Godspeed, and be thankful for every moment they were a part of our lives. The best shrine we can build to them is in our hearts.

Do not let your hearts be troubled. You believe in God; believe also in me. My Father's house has many rooms; if that were not so, would I have told you that I am going there to prepare a place for you? (John 14:1–2 NIV)

*Merciful and loving Father, we are thankful for the blessings that came into our lives through those with whose companionship we have been blessed, and who now reside in heaven with You. We pray that, until we join them, we will be attentive to the tasks that You set before us here on earth. We wait expectantly for the reward You have promised us, the reward our loved ones are even now enjoying. Through Christ our Redeemer, amen.*

# Five

# ACCEPTING THE COMMUNITY FACTOR

It's hard for most of us to lean on others. The bereaved often think, "No one can know how desolate I am, no one can understand what I'm going through, and no one can help me."

> *I've finally been able to make it through an entire church service without having to leave (although I still cry a lot, often at the least provocation). Last week's sermon, "The Community Factor," described how Christians lean on each other, and on God, for support in trying times. I was brought to tears by these words: "So many of you here today have sat in that same lonely place in the front pew to say good-bye to the love of your life, your best friend, and your soul mate. Every time I've heard your stories of five and six decades together, I've wondered, 'How do you go on living after that kind of loss?'" For forty years, Cynthia and I were partners, virtually inseparable, and her death has left me wondering the same thing. I can see now how it's possible for surviving spouses, separated from their soul mates of so many years, to feel as though there is absolutely no reason to go on living. I certainly do.*
>
> *When my pastor and I sat in the family room of the ICU*

*after Cynthia's death, he reminded me that, although as a physician I'd spent a great deal of my life ministering to others, it was time for me to let others minister to me. That's been hard to do, but, when I let them, my Christian friends and church family have been a significant source of support for me.*

*Cynthia's death will forever leave a hole in my life, a hole that will never be filled. And I've learned that those who suffer most in passing through the valley of the shadow of death are not those who go out the other side to a bright, heavenly home. It's those of us who are left behind who feel they are trapped in a box canyon. Each day, with God as my unseen guide, and with tangible support from my family of faith, I'm trying hard to break out of the darkness.* (Author's journal)

Accepting help from others—even realizing that help is needed—continues to be difficult for those in the midst of grief. To begin with, we believe no one can know the depth of our sorrow, the wrenching sense of loss we feel, the problems that continue to crop up day by day. We feel we can take as our theme song "Nobody Knows the Trouble I've Seen." What we fail to consider is the second line of that wonderful spiritual: "Nobody knows but Jesus."

Prayer is a wonderful source of comfort for the Christian. But frankly, most of us feel anger toward God for "letting this happen." The issue of why bad things happen to good people continues to be a source of theological argument, and the full answer is beyond the grasp of the average Christian, myself included. My view is that the pain of His children is shared by God, and although He doesn't necessarily intervene to stop bad things from happening, He can and does bring ultimate good out of those events. Sometimes we can eventually see this for ourselves, while in other situations His purpose may be revealed to us only in the light of eternity.

That having been said, I recommend that the hurting soul at least set aside periods for one-way prayer. If you can't talk to God, remain silent and open to His leading, and let Him talk to you. When even that is too much to bear, open the Bible to familiar passages of comfort, and let God's Word speak to your troubled heart. Begin with the Psalms, many of which cry out with anguish. While you're there, don't forget to read—often—the beautiful twenty-third Psalm, which speaks peace to the troubled heart.

God speaks to us not only in prayer and through the Bible but also through those with whom we share the common bond of brotherhood and sisterhood in Christ. In my church, the tangible evidence of concern at the time of loss often begins with an outpouring of food. When the heart is heavy, most of us don't want to eat, much less prepare food. We even think it's disrespectful to consider such mundane things at a time like this. Don't give way to this martyr complex, but rather maintain adequate nourishment, not only for general health but to avoid the accentuation of depression that comes with low blood sugar.

The grieving person needs to talk openly about the pain he or she is feeling. Take advantage of friends and church members who offer a sympathetic ear. There is healing and catharsis in talking things over, especially with someone you trust. Feel free to be yourself and to pour out your feelings, and don't worry about how your words or actions make you look in the eyes of others. True friends will listen nonjudgmentally and be supportive. Pastors and church staff can not only provide a listening ear and a shoulder to cry on but also help guide you through some of the roughest times. Many churches have a ministry with volunteers who have been equipped and trained to help in times like these. And finally, know that others have gone through a similar loss and are able to offer "been there, done that" advice and support.

The death of a loved one heals with a tender scar, which may always be sensitive. Healing is often slow, healing is sporadic, healing is sometimes incomplete, but, with God's help, healing is possible.

Share each other's burdens, and in this way obey the law of Christ. (Gal. 6:2)

∾

*Lord of all, thank You for the undergirding love of those who stand by us in our hour of deepest sorrow. May we never be hesitant or ashamed to reach out and claim their help, their support, and their love, which mirrors the love You have for all Your children. In Your name, amen.*

# FINDING A SUPPORT GROUP

After the death of a spouse, talking about it helps a great deal. And it's especially helpful to talk about your feelings and experiences with people who've been through the same thing. You may come in contact with these people through church, family, or friends, but there's a benefit to becoming part of a support group to whom you have previously been a total stranger—you can reveal your true feelings without having to dress them up or sugarcoat them.

*This morning, feeling very much like a kid being sent off to school when I didn't want to go, I drove to a local restaurant to meet with the widowed persons support group. We found each other mutually through my queries to the AARP and a website called WidowNet. Ann [my daughter] encouraged me to go, as did several of my friends. And, of course, it turned out to be fine. The ages represented range from late thirties to late fifties (plus me, at sixty-three), and today there were three women and three men in attendance. They had been widowed from five months to about a year, so I was not only the oldest person there but also the one freshest into the grieving process. For an hour, we talked, we shared experiences, we affirmed each other, and it was just a good chance to be with adults and have conversation without having to be afraid of what was said. I cried a bit (and I wasn't the only one), I laughed some (for the first time in ever so long), and just let my hair down and shared my feelings—how unmasculine, and how very helpful.* (Author's email to his children)

Humans need companionship. This very concept is validated by God's own Word, which tells us that after creating the first man, God recognized it was not good for the man to be alone. So He created a companion for him (Gen. 2:18). The loss of a spouse immediately takes away the in-house support group of one, upon which the survivor has been dependent for so long. Moreover, the deep emotions produced by the event, the difficult decisions that must be made, the changes in the life of the survivor—these things ordinarily would have been talked over with the very one who's no longer available.

You'll need to talk with your family and friends, pastor, and members of your church family. They will, no doubt, form the first line of your "support group," both for the acute situation and in the weeks and months that follow. But it's also helpful to find and become part of an active support group composed of persons who've been through experiences that mirror your own, and who will accept you without judging or criticizing anything you may share with them.

Many good and caring persons may surround you, but unless they've undergone the death of a spouse, they can't be as tuned in to the emotions and experiences you're going through as those who have suffered that loss. Those who have been there, done that can give you personal and practical advice on handling the things you're currently facing, often more so than can the most well-meaning person who hasn't had that firsthand experience.

In addition, most of us are hesitant to unburden ourselves and reveal emotions and actions that might be construed as selfish, weak, or inappropriate. This hesitancy is especially true when you're talking with those who are close to you: family, close friends, and even your pastor. We all want to be perceived as perfect, although we all know that none of us will ever come even close.

Research has shown that the best person to offer support to a widow is another widow (and the same obviously holds true for widowers). These are people who can truly say, "I know where you are—because I've been there too." Those in widow and widower groups can lift each other up by sympathizing, by advising, but, most of all, by letting each other talk, vent, cry, and let it all hang out.

For all these reasons, it's good to look for a specific support group outside your usual circles. One excellent place to start is online at www.WidowNet.org, a site devoted to persons whose spouses have died. In addition to discussion threads and information on meetings, the site has links to stories that deal with the unique problems of widows and widowers. Another avenue is through AARP, either through direct contact with the organization or through their website, especially the links found at www.aarp.org/families/grief_loss.

How long will you need the support group? The simple answer is "for as long as it takes." Some folks are able to move on more quickly than others, but there's no timetable for grief. As long as you're experiencing grief—whether on a daily basis, every few days, once a month, or when unexpected triggers occur—you should feel free to share it with fellow travelers along this road. And, after your journey has become smoother, don't discount the possibility that you may become an encourager to someone else whose journey has just begun. The road is long and difficult, but it is not without end, and it is better traveled with others than alone.

> Father to the fatherless, defender of widows—
>     this is God, whose dwelling is holy.
> God places the lonely in families.
>
> (Ps. 68:5–6)

*Loving God, You have promised never to give us more than we can bear. We depend on You to provide daily guidance, support, and grace for the difficult journey on which we find ourselves. Place people in our paths who will bear us up, direct our*

steps, and accept us, ignoring our frailties and our weaknesses. And when we have gained enough strength to make the journey on our own, don't let us forget the others who may need us to give to them what we have received. Thank You for Your provision of our needs. In Jesus's name, amen.

# Seven

# AVOIDING A
# SELF-CENTERED OUTLOOK

The loss of your loved one is felt by others as well, especially close family members. Although your resources for helping them may seem limited, getting outside your own grief for a while can be a good experience.

*I've talked with each of you tonight, and every conversation helped. Each and every one of you contains something of your mother, and I hope you appreciate that—I certainly do. I know that you care about me and, as a result, you "worry" a bit about me. I can assure you that certainly I've had a major change in my life, but I'm handling it about as well (maybe even better) than average—but even average is pretty bad in this situation. It's going to take patience and a willingness to allow time to pass, qualities that Cynthia recognized to be in short supply in my armamentarium, but which I'm beginning to develop. Thanks for being my support network, which is difficult enough while each of you is going through your own grief process. There is a Scripture verse Mom and I used to like to quote to each other, which (paraphrased) says, "Two are better than one, for if one shall fall, the other shall bear him up." Now it's your turn to bear me up, but I promise it's only for a while. In return, I hope each of you will feel free to call on me if you want to talk, to cry, to laugh, or just to make contact. It would probably help everyone concerned. Finally, know that I love and appreciate each of you so very much.* (Author's email to his children)

The person whose spouse passes away must endure strong emotions, which will probably remain intense for quite some time. If there are living children of the marriage, the parent who is left behind will also need to be supportive of these children, who have lost a parent. It's difficult to function effectively during the period immediately following the death of a spouse. For me, many actions were almost reflexive, dictated by "doing the right thing" and "doing what she would want." Few of us also have the emotional resources to be thoughtful and considerate of the needs and feelings of our children—the normal parental protective reflex—during that initial period of shock.

As time passes, however, the surviving parent will find it helpful to begin recognizing and reacting to the needs of others. This begins by checking on your children to see how they're recovering. For most of us, when our spouses die our children will be grown, living independently away from home. Realize their grief will be complicated by their concern for you. It's important to truthfully let them know how your own recovery is going. Be open and honest, but, insofar as you can do so, reassure them of your own progress. Among their emotions is not only grief for the lost parent but a disturbing realization; this death has brought home to them the cold truth that their parents are not immortal or invulnerable. They begin thinking, "I've lost one parent—how long will it be before I lose the other one?"

Younger children who have not left home and have been deprived of a parent at an early age present a different problem. This situation is much more difficult, and there is no set formula for dealing with it. Surviving parents must of necessity get outside themselves, putting aside their own grief to minister to the children. Physical needs must be met, the family unit requires someone at the helm to guide it, and plans for the future have to be made. Nevertheless, it's quite evident that the remaining parent will need time for his or her own grief, as well as the opportunity for rest and time alone during these trying days. Don't be hesitant to call on family members, friends, and your local church for help. There's no easy answer for the parent trying to be a source of strength to the children while inside feeling hollow, lost, and without direction. This is a case where getting outside yourself must be balanced with caring for yourself.

Being considerate toward your children is just one way in which you can avoid the trap of becoming a self-centered recluse whose primary emotion is summed up in two words: poor me. In the weeks and months after the death of a spouse, there may occur a similar loss among your circle of family and acquaintances. Although your initial inclination may be to avoid the person thus bereaved, you should realize your own experience has uniquely qualified you to be supportive and helpful to that person. True, there may be some emotional pain for you in reliving your own experience, but the end result is most often positive for all concerned.

Just a few months after the death of my wife, my brother-in-law died unexpectedly. I was asked to speak at the funeral service, and the preparation and delivery of that eulogy, plus going through the funeral experience itself, caused me to shed copious tears. My sister-in-law later told me, however, how much it meant to her to have me walk beside her in her grief. God may place someone in your path for you to walk beside, using your tragedy in a positive fashion. Don't turn your back on the opportunity, even though it presents a challenge.

Finally, there will come a time when your own wounds will have healed sufficiently to allow you to more easily console, counsel, and encourage others who have suffered the death of their spouses. This opportunity may come through a widowed persons support group, through the Stephen Ministry of a church, or in some other fashion. I encourage you always to be aware that, as a widow or widower, you are a member of an exclusive group, one in which membership is never sought but which will come to one spouse or the other when death takes their partner. Use your experience to lighten the burdens of your brothers and sisters, and you'll find your load lighter at the end of the day.

> Dear children, let's not merely say that we love each other; let us show the truth by our actions. (1 John 3:18)

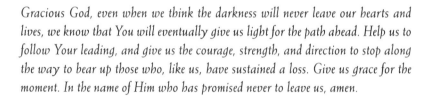

*Gracious God, even when we think the darkness will never leave our hearts and lives, we know that You will eventually give us light for the path ahead. Help us to follow Your leading, and give us the courage, strength, and direction to stop along the way to bear up those who, like us, have sustained a loss. Give us grace for the moment. In the name of Him who has promised never to leave us, amen.*

# Eight

# RESIGNING YOUR COMMISSIONS

Marriage involves looking out for each other. It's hard to give this up, even after the death of your spouse.

*I'm weary, and sort of punch-drunk, after a six-hundred-mile drive from South Padre Island. Brian [our son] helped me arrange for Coast Guard assistance in scattering Cynthia's ashes there, a place that meant so much for us. While I stewed for three days in a motel room, waiting for weather to clear, I tried so hard to plan things perfectly. When our launch finally was able to put out to sea, the station executive officer told me that there's no standard burial-at-sea service in the Blue Jackets Manual, and asked if I wanted him to turn back and get a chaplain. Instead, I did the service myself, quoting from memory the passage from Romans I had chosen for Cynthia's memorial service, ending with the assurance that nothing, not even death, can separate us from the love of God. After committing her ashes to the sea, I sat and cried all the way back to the shore. But I think Cynthia would have been pleased, and it just seemed right for me to step in and do one last thing for her—I've had over forty years' practice, and it's going to be hard to stop. (Author's journal)*

*I've made a profound discovery. For forty-three years, three as a couple and forty as husband and wife, I have felt the self-imposed pressure to do what was best for Cynthia, to do what would please her, to take care of her. After her death, in my daily prayers, I have continued to pray for assurance that she is safe, happy, and in God's care. It hit me yesterday that if I truly believe what I've been saying all these years, I have assurance that it's a given that she is indeed all that. And what I need to do is resign my job of protector/caregiver/husband and let it go. I have to assume that God will keep His end of the bargain. I know that she more than kept hers.* (Author's journal)

Habits are easy to form and hard to break. Over decades of marriage, it's easy to fall into routines of action, even habitual thought patterns. One of these is the habit of taking care of your spouse, something that becomes unconscious over the years. When you make even the simplest decision, you automatically factor in what he or she would think of the action. Without conscious thought, you approach situations with the unstated goal of not creating hardship for your partner. And always in the forefront of your mind is the reflex to be protective.

When you are no longer two but one, even though your actions and their consequences no longer affect your spouse, it's hard to break the habits of a lifetime. In the days and weeks that follow the death of your beloved, there are many opportunities to protect him or her. This protection begins with the obituary. There's a real temptation to take on a commission as press agent. You want everyone to know all the merits and accomplishments of this person and to realize the world will be a duller, less complete place without him or her. You want to be certain nothing is left out that might attest to the person's deeds and worth. It's as though you were introducing this person with whom you shared your life and want to be certain the world is duly impressed.

At some point, you will be able to look back and realize that your spouse wrote his or her own obituary in the hearts of family members, friends, and the community. What is written in the newspaper, or what is said in the eulogy at the memorial service, won't last in the memory of those who read or hear it. What is enduring are the examples that were set, the acts of kindness and love that were committed, the way in which a life was lived. This testament was written long before the obituary was set down on paper, and it will last much longer. Rather than giving yourself an ulcer over whether you left out anything important in the composition of a memorial piece, recognize the impermanence of those words. Consider the more permanent memorials that were constructed years ago: happy memories made with a grandchild, trips to the store for a neighbor who was ill, and a joyful voice in the choir.

A similar job you may need to resign is that of chief architect of monuments. Let me give you an example. There's nothing wrong with looking at a well-kept garden or beautiful flowers and saying, "My spouse did that." But if your mate had a green thumb, and yours is permanently brown, your efforts to make that garden an everlasting monument to your departed spouse are doomed to produce frustration and to end in failure. Cynthia was an avid gardener, deriving a great deal of joy from it, and was able to make almost any plant grow and flourish. As you might expect, when I was left to handle all those flower beds, those bushes and shrubs, and the garden, my first reaction was to delve into all her gardening books in a frantic effort to keep everything alive and looking wonderful. When a plant died, it was as though I was experiencing her death all over again. This went on for months, until her brother, a farmer, reacted to my expression of anguish by saying, "They're just plants." They may have been planted and nurtured by my late wife, but if they had died while under her care, she would have merely pulled them up and gone about her business. In the end, with help, I've managed to make our flower beds attractive but low-maintenance. This doesn't detract from my memories of Cynthia's magic with flowers. I've just chosen to resign my self-appointed commission to carry forward that torch.

The monument you are trying to maintain might not be flowers, but something else your husband or wife left behind. Don't feel you have dishonored your spouse by not carrying on his or her work. Another good piece of advice came from my oldest son when I told him I'd decided to eventually sell the farmland that Cynthia had loved (and I had tolerated). He simply said, "Dad, the worst thing you could ever do would be to try to keep living Mom's life for her." I commend that advice to each of you, whatever your circumstances.

Finally, like me, you may be led to pray repeatedly for God to take care of your departed loved one. I derived comfort in doing this (as well as feeling proud of my obvious spirituality) until it dawned on me that I was asking God to do what He had already promised to carry out. My time and effort would be better spent praying for strength, guidance, comfort, and grace for myself and for all the loved ones left behind. So, after an embarrassingly long time, I resigned that last commission. Now my prayers contain thanks for the assurance that Cynthia has gone to be with the Lord and for the promise that the same reward awaits me, as it does all those who call on the name of our Savior.

> Jesus answered him, "Truly I tell you, today you will be with me in paradise." (Luke 23:43 NIV)

> For just as the new heavens and new earth
>     that I am making will stand firm before me . . .
> So will your children
>     and your reputation stand firm.
> (Isa. 66:22 MSG)

❧

*Loving Father, it's so hard to let go. It's hard not to try to keep our loved ones alive in the hearts of others, since they are still so much in ours. Help us see that they have gone on to something so much better than anything we can imagine, and may we be thankful for the reward they have now claimed and that someday awaits us. Until that day, heal our hurting hearts and guide our faltering steps. In our Savior's name, amen.*

# Nine

# TACKLING THE PUZZLE
# OF PRAYER

As Christians we are taught to pray—to pray for the sick, to approach God in faith, to believe in the power of prayer. But what are we to believe when bad things happen despite our prayers to the contrary? Do the prayers of others really help those who grieve?

*I am realizing that the prayers of others are important. One of the consequences of my palpable anger with God, which filled me when it became obvious that Cynthia as I knew her had ceased to exist, was that it was exceedingly difficult to pray. Oh, I know that at the lunch served before the memorial service, I asked the blessing myself (because I thought it was the right thing to do, in my role as head of the family—the patriarch), and although I'm sure the words sounded good, the spirit behind them was hollow. Since Cynthia's death, I have tried to pray several times daily, and although sometimes the prayers are no more than, "Why, God?" I believe that the continuing experience is helping me rebuild a bridge of trust and love back to Him. It's also more and more apparent to me that during all this time I've been supported by the prayers of others. Family, friends, church groups, and many, many others—all praying not only for Cynthia while there was still hope but now for me and for the rest of the family. I never appreciated the power of prayer when I was the one doing the praying—but when we are the ones being prayed for, whether we know it or not, it makes a huge difference. I will never again feel the same way about praying for others, after having been on the other end of that lifeline.* (Author's journal)

"We're praying for you." How many times have you heard those words? You respond with a sincere "Thank you," happy that others care enough about you to intercede with God on your behalf. But what is your attitude about the prayers that are offered? If the life of your loved one hung in the balance for any time at all, you and many others offered prayers for his or her recovery. How do you feel, knowing that these prayers didn't yield the result you desired?

When a loved one is critically ill, it's natural and normal to pray for healing, for restoration of health, and for the opportunity to hold on to him or her for a while longer. But these prayers must be offered with the full realization that such intervention may not be forthcoming. A petition for strength, for grace, for comfort, and for guidance in the face of whatever tragedy may await us should accompany petitions for healing. Remember that Christ, when praying to His Father while anticipating the agony of His crucifixion, began by praying, "Father . . . everything is possible for you. Please take this cup of suffering away from me." But He followed that immediately with the prayer of surrender, "Yet I want your will to be done, not mine" (Mark 14:36).

It's hard to pray with faith that can move mountains when we realize our prayers may not yield the results we desire. We sometimes blame God for "letting" bad things happen. The truth of the matter is, we don't know the mind of God. We don't understand why suffering has to occur. We can't believe that a loving Father wouldn't intervene. Is God even out there? Does He care?

When our prayers for healing don't appear to bear fruit, are we to assume that we're not good enough? Does the person whose life we pray so earnestly for fail to measure up to the standard God has set? Is there significance to the circumstance when one person is spared and another dies, despite prayers that are offered up on every hand?

God grieves alongside His children when tragedy strikes. He doesn't cause these tragic events. Death is one of the by-products of man's fall from the perfection of creation. Although God permits it, He takes no joy in it. Once the train of free will was in motion, God took His hand off the throttle—but He didn't get off the train.

There is hope, nevertheless, for the power of prayer. God has promised that nothing will befall His children that is beyond their power to bear. He assures us that He will walk with us, guide us, undergird us, and be with us through the valleys of despair. It is this very company and comfort that is sometimes the fruit of prayers that have been offered to stave off a tragedy. There's nothing wrong with praying for healing. We should continue to do so. But these prayers must be combined with the acceptance of our inability to understand God's greater purpose, and a plea that, whatever the outcome, we will be given comfort, guidance, and direction. That's what God has really promised us. And He keeps that promise.

> The eternal God is your refuge,
> and his everlasting arms are under you.
> (Deut. 33:27)

*Loving and caring Father, we acknowledge that we cannot discern Your plan for our lives and those of our loved ones. We continue to pray that Your Holy Spirit would walk beside us to comfort and to guide, and that You would use even tragedies to further Your good purpose in our lives and the lives of those around us. We trust You, even when we don't understand. In Your strong name, amen.*

*Ten*

# OVERCOMING FRUSTRATION

God hasn't promised that things will always work out the way we plan or desire. But He has pledged to help us get through tough times, whether or not we can see a reason for what has happened or agree with the outcome.

*For the past three days, I've been especially prone to crying for no real reason—the simplest thing can trigger a memory and set me off. Maybe all this crying is good for me. I hope so. For two weeks while Cynthia was in ICU, I held myself together by sheer willpower so that I could be there with her, and then after she passed away I continued to hold myself together to get through the memorial service and things that had to be done right away. I guess now is when it really hits. I keep asking myself, "Why did this happen?"*

*Our pastor told me that grief doesn't really come in nice, discrete stages—it comes in waves (each of which may contain several stages), and he was right. But I've also found that, with the passage of time, the waves don't always last as long or reach as high (or low), and I continue to hope the seas will eventually calm. I can't see rhyme or reason to Cynthia's death, and maybe I won't be able to until I stand before God. Until then, I just have to trust Him. . . . I don't see any other way to get through this.* (Author's email to Cynthia's siblings)

In the days, weeks, and months after the death of a husband or wife, the survivor can expect to experience periods of grief and absolute desolation, and a deep sense of loss, all of which can be devastating. There is no predicting when these periods will come, how long they will last, and to what degree they will prevent any semblance of normal functioning. But it is absolutely certain that they will come. And they will be accompanied by anger at God and doubts about His plan for us.

During these dark periods, one of the thoughts that continues to come unbidden into the grieving mind is, "Why did God do this?" Or, if we're able to get our minds around the concept that God doesn't arbitrarily cause bad things to happen, we ask, "Why did God allow this?" We live in a world where seeming injustices and inequities are a part of daily living. People die every day, many of them taken by violence long before the end of their expected life spans. Some die of cancer and other diseases, perhaps lingering in pain or laboring under handicaps. Does God actually plan for these and so many other terrible things to happen?

This question has been asked since Old Testament times, when Job's "comforters" repeatedly asked him what he had done to cause God to punish him. Surely the loss of his material possessions, the death of his children, and the development of a painful physical affliction could only come as punishment from a righteous God. Job's answer speaks volumes for his faith. He doesn't understand the whys and wherefores. He just knows that God has an eventual plan, so, rather than cursing his God, Job continues to praise Him. We all learned in Sunday school that Job's faithfulness was rewarded by God, and things were put right. What bothers those of us who have suffered the death of a spouse is that God hasn't reached down and put things right for us. We don't understand how or why this happened, and, because we don't see an end to the suffering and inequity that these circumstances produce, it tests our faith as surely as Job's afflictions tested his.

I accept the fact that God is truly all-powerful and all-knowing, able to perform miracles whenever and however He chooses. I've come to the realization, however, that I will never in this world and within the confines of my own humanity be able to understand God's plan as it affects my life and that of others around me. I cannot successfully argue with God about why He spared this person and not that one, why my wife died and someone else's mate lived. Yet I feel a firm assurance that, someday, I and my Christian brothers and sisters will understand the reasons behind events that we now find incomprehensible. For now, all you and I can do is continue to pray for grace for the moment and a revelation of God's continuing will for us, day by day.

> I have told you these things, so that in Me you may have [perfect] peace. In the world you have tribulation and distress and suffering, but be courageous [be confident, be undaunted, be filled with joy]; I have overcome the world. [My conquest is accomplished, My victory abiding.] (John 16:33 AMP)

~

*All-powerful and all-knowing God, we are frustrated because of apparently senseless events that rob us of our loved ones and put doubt into our minds about Your caring for us. Teach us once more that we cannot in this world know the ins and outs of Your plans for us, and help us to wait patiently on You. Give us grace for the moment, day by day, until someday we see fully revealed what You have prepared for us and for those loved ones who are already enjoying the fruits of their labors. In Your precious name, amen.*

# Eleven

# CHANGING YOUR WAY
# OF THINKING

The loss of a spouse causes us to change many things. This should include making an effort to change the way we think about ourselves.

> *I discovered more of Cynthia's papers in a nightstand the other night. Included were notes from a grief seminar she attended at one of her nurses' meetings. The discussion of the initial stages of shock, emotional lability, depression, guilt, resentment, and anger are followed by the notation "hope arrives." Then in capital letters she wrote, CHANGE YOUR WAY OF THINKING! I'm trying, but it's not easy.*
>
> *As I go through the house, straightening and cleaning, everything reminds me of her. We did so many neat things together over the years, and part of my grief centers around the fact that she isn't around to share with anymore. I look at the sunset, and turn to comment on it, but she's not there. I hear a bit of news, and think "Cynthia would like to hear that," but she's not there for me to tell. I see an ad for a movie, and think, "Maybe we'll see that." But there's no more "we."*
> (Author's journal)

For so many years, you were part of an "us." You agreed that God knew what He was doing when He said, "It is not good that man should be alone." You were there for each other, to offer support, to talk things out, to laugh and to cry together, to share. Now suddenly, you're alone. You see a beautiful sunset and automatically turn to your companion to share the sight—and you are alone. You come upon a beautiful passage in a book and begin to read it aloud to your companion—and realize you are alone. You fill out one of the forms that mark everyday life, and when you begin to check the M in the "marital status" box, it hits you once more—you now must check W. So much has changed. And you have to change too. You must change your way of thinking.

The world is made for couples. You never think about it when you're part of that world but, now that you're single again, you see that you've become a fifth wheel. For a while after your bereavement, friends invite you out to dinner or to other social functions, but these often are uncomfortable situations. How many times in the past in similar functions did you depend on your spouse or companion for rescue from conversations that were boring or uncomfortable? Now you're stuck. And you sense (often correctly) that the folks engaging you in such conversation would probably rather be talking to other couples but feel it's their duty to cheer you up. No one wins in these situations.

You come to dread walking into your favorite restaurant and hearing the phrase, "Just one?" So you stop going to your favorite restaurant. Besides, too many memories are associated with the place, memories of happier times, reminding you that's all come to an end. You've been a member of a couple's class at church for years, and now you're no longer a couple. Your friends are supportive, but again you find yourself feeling like an outsider. And, in the midst of all this, is the unexplainable feeling of guilt at having somehow departed from the norm, for being less than is expected of you because you're without a partner.

There's no need to belabor the point—your status has changed. The important question is, *what do you do about it?* The answer is simple to say, hard to carry out: change your way of thinking. Change the rules you've set for yourself. Be prepared to ignore the rules you've come to accept from society about single persons. Change your priorities to include making yourself happy. Begin to think of yourself as an individual, not as part of a couple. Is this disrespectful of your departed loved one? Think about it. Would he or she want you to perpetually mourn and sequester yourself from society, or would your spouse be pleased if you once more found happiness in your life? You know the answer.

It becomes a habit for couples to consider their actions based on their effect on each other. Such consideration is wonderful, and makes a marriage work more smoothly. Now, the test is no longer, "What is the effect on my companion?" but "What is the effect on me?" If you never watched a certain TV program or attended certain types of movies because your spouse or companion didn't care for them, change your way of thinking. Make a conscious effort to tailor your actions to suit yourself, and only yourself. If you avoided activities because they appealed only to you, and you didn't want to be selfish, now's the time to consider them once again. In other words, begin to think in terms of "I," not "we."

Don't just sit at home and eat TV dinners. They're often the first course at a full-blown pity party. Take along a good book, walk into your favorite restaurant, and firmly say, "Table for one, please." If the maître d' asks, "Just one?" and you're feeling particularly devilish, answer, "Yes, unless you'd like to join me." If you don't want to read while you eat, just look around. People watching is a great way to pass time in a public place. You'll see couples dining who never have two words to say to each other during the meal. What a waste! You'll be sad, thinking, "If I only had that chance again." But don't let it deter you. Get out regularly if you can afford it. It'll be good for you.

By this time, you're beginning to get the picture. As much as it hurts, as much as it reminds you that you're no longer part of a couple, you must begin thinking of yourself as single. But that doesn't mean you have to suffer endlessly because of it. The responsibility for making you happy now rests squarely on your own shoulders.

Will you ever be part of a couple again? For most of you reading this book, it may be too soon to even think about that. Whether you continue to live alone, or once again become part of a couple, your current task can be described very simply: change your way of thinking. The rest is in God's hands.

> Why are you in despair, O my soul?
> And why have you become disturbed within me?
> Hope in God, for I shall again praise Him
> For the help of His presence.
>
> (Ps. 42:5 NASB)

~

*Father of us all, our loss makes us all the more dependent on You. Teach us to love ourselves, as You love us, and help us to make the difficult transition to being one, instead of half of a couple. Walk with us, sustain us, and lead us through sorrow to the rebuilding of our lives. In Your healing name, amen.*

# Twelve

# EXPANDING YOUR HORIZONS

There's a danger that you'll become a prisoner of the past for the indefinite future. One very real aspect of the healing process is the ability to get beyond what you did as a couple, to get out of the routines that guided your life for so many years, and to think of a future without your partner. A failure to do so may characterize a widow or widower who will continue to be that prisoner of the past.

> *I'm trying so hard to get on with my life. I'm back teaching and lecturing, and that means travel. I've almost reached the point where I can walk into a hotel room and not cry because I'm alone. I always find myself wanting to point out things to you and share them. Actually, I still do, but now just in my mind.*
>
> *I've contracted with a nursery to maintain the flower beds and gardens. I just don't have your touch (and I really don't get the enjoyment out of it that you did). I hated to spend the money on myself, but I finally bought new clubs and am back playing golf again. I'm afraid that most of my meals are still defrosted and cooked in the microwave, and are eaten in front of the TV—I just can't get interested in going out alone. I know there's a life out there without you, but right now I just don't have the inclination to look for it. I miss you, Darling, and I*

*guess I always will. But I can just hear you saying to me what you always said when I was going to play golf, or work out at the athletic club, or watch a football game: "Enjoy." I'll try . . . but it's hard.* (Author's letter to Cynthia written after her death)

What was your spouse's favorite form of recreation? Was it gardening, golf, fishing, reading, travel? Some couples enjoyed these things together, while for others what was wonderfully relaxing and pleasant for one held no interest for the other. Marriage is made up of ongoing compromises: if one of you wanted to see the Grand Canyon and the other considered it just a big hole in the ground, that trip probably still got made. If your spouse worked constantly in the garden, as did Cynthia, there were probably times when you worked there too, even though you'd rather be doing something else.

In the weeks and months following the death of a spouse, the remaining partner may find herself or himself continuing to respond to guidelines and boundaries that no longer exist. Your actions have heretofore been linked to the likes and dislikes of your mate. Perhaps your husband or wife was ill or disabled for a significant period before death. Those constraints are no longer placed on your life, but there's a real likelihood you'll continue to function with that mind-set until you make a conscious effort to do otherwise.

Cynthia was in a coma in the intensive care for two weeks before her death. A few weeks after she died, as I attempted to regain some degree of normalcy, I realized that I needed to get away, to clear my mind, to rest, and to give vent to the emotions I continued to feel. We had always enjoyed South Padre Island, but when the notion of traveling there came to mind, my first reaction was, "Can I do that?" Only by sitting down and consciously thinking through my new situation could I convince myself that the major deciding factor, now and henceforth, was going to be, "Would I enjoy it?" Then I had to convince myself that enjoying myself was neither out of place with the grief I was feeling nor disrespectful of Cynthia. Doing so was difficult, but it was necessary to the coping process.

These types of changes affect not just your plans for travel or recreation. Was there a food not served in your home because your spouse didn't care for it? If it's something you like, reintroduce it into your diet. Were there movies you didn't see because he or she had different tastes? Treat yourself to a weekday matinee. Did you avoid activities because you didn't want to be away from your mate? Make plans to enjoy them. It may be golf, fishing, gardening, reading, writing, painting—it's time to begin thinking about what the new normal is going to be. It will be different, and it's often hard to think of pleasing just yourself, but the sooner you begin doing this, the sooner you'll start the slow escape from the morass of grief, depression, and self-pity that enfolds each of us who have suffered the death of a husband or wife.

Realize that the process of grieving does not involve depriving yourself of all future pleasures. Denying yourself pleasure, making a fetish of self-sacrifice, and discontinuing all your old normal activities won't make your loss any more palatable. Nor will it signal to those around you how genuine your grief is. These actions and attitudes simply hold you more firmly in the snare of depression that waits for all who mourn. Instead, look around and see the areas where you can do something for yourself, something you might not have dreamed of doing in the past. Expand your horizons and explore your options, or you may find yourself trapped in the downward spiral of grief and self-pity that enfolds so many widows and widowers. Remember, your departed loved one would undoubtedly be the first to give you the same command that Cynthia gave me so often: "Enjoy."

> His anger lasts only a moment,
>     but his favor lasts a lifetime!
> Weeping may last through the night,
>     but joy comes with the morning. . . .
> You have turned my mourning into joyful dancing.
>     You have taken away my clothes of mourning and
>         clothed me with joy.
>
> (Ps. 30:5, 11)

*Loving Father, we don't want things to be different; we want them to be back the way they were. Help us to accept the changes in our lives. We pray that You will show us how to love ourselves, as our departed spouses loved us, and that we will seek and find the new normal for our lives. In the midst of our grief and sorrow, grant us moments of joy, because joy is what You have in store for each of us in the fullness of Your time. In Your blessed name, amen.*

*Thirteen*

# PUTTING FLOWERS
# ON THE GRAVE

The bereaved spouses will soon find a place where they feel closest to their departed mates. It may be at the gravesite, in a garden, or following the route of their daily walks. This normal and natural part of the grieving process can be healthy, if done with the right attitude.

> *For most of our married life, Cynthia gardened. She happily toiled, planting trees, shrubs, and flowers. Her favorite activity for the last years of her life was to work at the acreage we had bought just south of town, a spot in the country where she could plant and cultivate to her heart's content. We were going to spend our retirement years there, but she died before that could become a reality. Because Cynthia was cremated and her ashes scattered over the Gulf of Mexico, there is no gravesite for me to visit. But I soon discovered that walking among the trees and flowers on the farmland she loved rekindled her memory in my heart. This was the place where I sensed her spirit. For me, visiting the farm is like visiting her grave.*
>
> *For quite a while after Cynthia's death, visits to the farm*

*ended in tears and a sense of depression. Little by little I'm finding that it's peaceful to go there, tend the flowers and bushes, walk the land, let my mind wander. I always feel closer to Cynthia when I leave, and I guess that's progress.* (Author's email to a friend)

The act of visiting a grave can be very beneficial. Keeping the site clean and bringing flowers to the grave are traditional ways to honor the one buried there. On these visits, talking with the departed spouse is a natural outgrowth of a long relationship—each knew the other so well one could usually finish the other's sentences. If, for whatever reason, there is no grave, it may be good to find somewhere meaningful to both the departed and the bereaved where you can meditate, pray, and even talk with your loved one. All these actions help ease the pain you feel as you come to the realization that the companionship that was once such an integral part of your life has now ended.

As with most things in life, these visits can be carried to an unhealthy extreme. The spouse or other grieving person who feels an irresistible need to visit the grave every day may be unconsciously denying the finality of the loss. He or she may feel that, through these visits, contact with the loved one may be kept alive indefinitely, and that the departed will never truly be lost. Rather, these visits (with whatever frequency they occur) should be the occasion for recalling the positives of our relationships with the deceased, while helping us to recognize the finality of the acute loss. The blow of this loss can be softened by reading Scriptures that remind us that, for the Christian, death is simply a way station on the road to eternal life. During the visit is also a good time and place for meditative prayer.

The funeral is traditionally a time to celebrate the life of the departed, but its major psychological function is to help those left behind come to grips with loss. Visiting the gravesite can continue this process. It should be done, not out of a sense of duty or in a futile attempt to deny the loss of the loved one, but to use the physical setting to remind us of the good moments we enjoyed with our lost

loved ones and to look forward to a joyous reunion in heaven someday. For the Christian, the grave is not a monument to death, but the
entrance to new life—life eternal.

> You build tombs for the prophets and decorate the graves of
> the righteous. (Matt. 23:29 NIV)

*Lord Jesus, who triumphed over death and the grave, help us to see our earthly loss
in perspective. Continue to give us wonderful memories of times we enjoyed with our
loved ones. May the tears we shed for our acute loss turn to joy when we consider
the bliss that awaits each of us in heaven, bliss that our departed loved ones enjoy
even now. In Your eternal name, amen.*

*Fourteen*

# PLAYING BACK THE "SCRIPTS"

There are situations in which the bereaved spouse feels especially close to the departed loved one. When this happens, it's not unusual to engage in a one-sided conversation. It's amazing how often the "scripts" of conversations stored up over many years together will turn a monologue into a dialogue.

> *I went to the farm property today. I checked all the trees and plants, and they were fine. Then I walked the property, the way we both used to. I used this opportunity (please don't start commitment papers on me yet) to talk aloud with Cynthia. I said I wished I could be certain that she is happy and at peace, asked forgiveness if I failed in anything I did to care for her in her last days, and in general just had a good cry. And, just as though she were there, I sensed the answer, "Dear, I'm fine. I'm more worried about you. Stop fretting about things you can't control or change. Learn to enjoy life the way I did. And while you're out here, it wouldn't hurt to mow the dead wildflowers so they'll reseed better next spring. And don't forget to fill the bird feeders." So I did . . . and I felt better.* (Author's email to his children)

No matter how many or how few years you were together, the habit of talking with your spouse and bouncing ideas off each other was

58

quickly formed and is slowly broken. Now you're on your own. You have friends and family to whom you can talk, but there isn't anyone who knows you so intimately as your spouse did. With your husband or wife, you didn't have to lay the groundwork for a conversation or explain the background of a decision. He or she knew your family finances and was aware of your likes and dislikes, and you could talk about past events without having to set the stage and explain what went before. Now all that has changed. You're on your own.

Psychologists talk about scripts that play in our heads—words and concepts implanted long ago from our parents, our spouses, our friends. We don't, of course, carry around actual devices that play these messages at the appropriate time. All believers, for example, will, from time to time, think back on what they learned through Bible study, from sermons and Sunday school lessons, and through the witness of Christian friends, and thus be guided in their actions.

So while the concept isn't new, the application is different for bereaved spouses. We too have knowledge gained by experience—knowledge of what our departed spouses would probably advise us to say or do. When indecision has you stumped, try a one-sided conversation with your mate. Imagine talking about your quandary. Think back to similar situations, and remember how they were handled. This is not a foolproof or guaranteed solution, but you'll be surprised how often one of those scripts starts playing, and you can almost hear his or her voice providing insight for you. Cynthia and I were married for forty years, and more than one friend commented over the years that we seemed joined at the hip. Indeed, we were very close, although our personalities and viewpoints were often different. Over the years, I learned to see and to respect her view, as she did mine. Now when I have one of these one-sided conversations, it helps me to see things from a different perspective, and sometimes it reminds me to take a different approach.

I'm certainly not saying that this practice will bring back your loved one or even solve all your problems. It will, however, often remind you of how you were able to bear each other's burdens, and it will prove the truth of the old adage that "two heads are better than one." Certainly, when faced with a difficult decision, you should pray, as well as seek counsel from family and close friends when it is appropriate. But don't sell short the benefit of seeking a quiet place and having a one-sided conversation.

> Go stand at the crossroads and look around.
> Ask for directions to the old road,
> The tried-and-true road. Then take it.
> Discover the right route for your souls.
> (Jer. 6:16 MSG)

*Father, when our lives are in turmoil, help us to step back and quiet our hearts. We thank You for the time, however long or short, that we had with our loved ones who are now with You. Help us to draw on that experience, just as we lean on You, when we feel alone and confused. We know that You want us to find and to travel the right road, and we thank You for Your love that sends us along that path. In the name of Jesus, our guide, amen.*

# Fifteen

# FINDING SOMEONE TO TALK TO

The death of a spouse takes away the opportunity for daily conversation. Whether trivial or profound, those conversations have been shared for years. Finding an acceptable outlet and substitute is difficult but necessary.

> *Sorry to bend your ear so much. I talk with the kids almost daily, but I just don't feel I can unload on them every time we talk. I have friends who call me, but none of them know me like you do, and I can't really unburden myself to them about some things. I miss Cynthia so . . . I'd give anything to talk with her again.* (Author's email to a friend)

> *I don't know how many more of these letters will come. I'm emailing a lot of folks, but some of this I'm not ready to share with anyone. I guess that's what I miss the most—the fact that for so long we were essentially one person, and sharing didn't always involve talking. Just being together was enough. And when we did need to talk, we were always there for each other.* (Author's letter to Cynthia written after her death)

The grief that stems from the death of a spouse is even more difficult to endure because we've lost the very one to whom we turned for so many years to talk out our disappointments and calamities. As discussed in the previous chapter, prolonged "conversations" with the departed loved one are not uncommon in the weeks and months after his or her death, especially when many years together have given the survivor the ability to accurately predict the other side of the dialogue. But you also need communication with a living person. Having a shoulder to cry on is a necessity. Being able to tell someone how bereft you feel, how unfair life is, how distanced from God you seem to be, becomes a need that must be met. To whom can, and should, the grieving person turn?

The natural instinct of any parent is to protect his or her children from undue suffering. To this end, after the loss of a spouse, many widows and widowers are very careful not to take their troubles to their adult children. The bereaved recognizes that his or her children are grieving for their own loss, and hesitates to add worry about their surviving parent to those burdens. Conversely, children often hide the depth of their grief in order to spare the feelings of their surviving parent. The result is a two-way charade that fails to help any of the parties involved. Parents and children should not hesitate to communicate their feelings as part of the mutual support needed at this time. But the expectations of this exchange should be realistic. Although voicing one's anguish may and probably will be therapeutic for the moment, neither a listening ear nor a comforting hug is likely to immediately produce relief from loneliness, bitterness, and a sense of loss. This will come with the passage of time. In the acute situation, either parent or child should feel free to say, "I'm feeling thus-and-so," and the other can truly reply, "I know, I feel it too," each expressing grief to the other without the burden of trying to make each other well again. Just knowing that someone cares about and understands their grief and sense of loss is important.

Other family members may provide a means for unburdening oneself. Siblings, in-laws, cousins, and others may provide a sounding board and listening ear. Realize that the closer to the deceased they are, the more likely that they are feeling similar grief. The same rules should apply as for parent and child—let's share our feelings, knowing we cannot shoulder the responsibility for providing the peace that only God can bring with time.

Close friends are often the best sources for bereaved persons to unburden themselves. In many instances, it is easier to be honest and open with our emotions to friends than to family members. We somehow feel that with family we must present the facade expected of us. With our friends, we more often tend to honestly and openly declare how we are feeling, even if we aren't putting up a brave front and handling it well.

A special situation arises when talking with a pastor, a member of the church staff, or even acquaintances from church. One of the stages of grief is anger, and although this anger is sometimes directed at the loved one who "left us," anger with and estrangement from God are also very typical as a result of such a loss. Yet bereaved Christians often feel the need to voice platitudes and declare their faith at such times, even when our hearts are crying out in agony. A Christian counselor needs the insight that allows him or her to assure the bereaved person that feelings of anger are normal, and even though that person may withdraw from God, God remains near to the bereaved person and will be with that person through the process of grief and recovery. Although Job was able to bear his losses and suffering without cursing God (as his "comforters" suggested that he do), most of us are all too human and un-Job-like when faced with such a major loss as the death of a spouse or close loved one.

Talking helps the process of grieving, and it can supply the human contact and care so necessary for the one who is suffering.

> Listen to my words, LORD,
>     consider my lament.
> Hear my cry for help,
>     my King and my God,
>     for to you I pray.
> In the morning, LORD, you hear my voice;

in the morning I lay my requests before you
and wait expectantly.

(Ps. 5:1–3 NIV)

∾

*Compassionate Father, help us to realize You are there for us, even when we feel far from You. Put in our paths friends and caring family members who will listen, who will dialogue with us, who will love us when we feel and act so very unlovely, and who will walk at our sides through the valley of despair that overshadows us. In Your name, amen.*

# Sixteen

# THROWING AWAY THE CARDS

How typical it is to keep things when common sense tells us they have no earthly use. Bereaved survivors are frequently unwilling to let go of any tangible reminders of their lost loved ones, even the sympathy cards and letters.

*This morning I went to the back of a closet where, for two years, I've kept a huge cardboard box. It's filled with all the sympathy cards, cards from flowers, notifications of memorial donations, and published tributes to Cynthia, all of which I've collected since her death. I hadn't looked at them since writing thank-you notes after the funeral, or when I was notified of memorial contributions. But I couldn't throw them away until now.*

*Today, I scanned through the addresses on the cards and was reminded of how many lives Cynthia touched in a positive way, and how much she contributed to this world in the short sixty-two years allotted to her. After her death, I felt an urge to be sure that she wasn't "forgotten." In my mind, keeping these tangible reminders was one way to do that. Besides that, for the longest time after her death, I couldn't look at the box, much less the cards, without crying.*

*With the clarity that two years bring, I'm able to recognize that Cynthia constructed a lasting and living memorial during her lifetime through everything she did. What I had been doing by trying to make sure she was "remembered" was not only redundant, it was almost insulting to imply that she needed further memorializing. To keep these cards had been my way of "building a monument to grief." So I consigned them to the recycle bin. Cynthia would have been proud of me for recycling.* (Author's journal)

I didn't throw away anything important that was connected with Cynthia. I just validated the fact that God keeps score differently than we do. When we begin to accept that, we're not cleaning house, we're moving on.

After the death of a husband or wife, it's gratifying to receive sympathy cards. This is a tangible assurance that people share in your grief and sense of loss. The same can be said of floral tributes, whether flowers and wreaths displayed at a memorial service or plants delivered to your home. It's important (or at least it was for me) to know that the life of our spouse had an impact on other people, and somehow it seems to validate the worth of the time they were with us before their death.

Phone calls are also important, but in my experience these are scarcer than the cards. I suppose that's because most people really don't know what to say when they call. It's so much easier to write, "You're in our prayers" or "Let us know what we can do." But that's not to demean friends who write rather than call. Every expression of sympathy, indeed every human contact, is important during the time when loss is felt most acutely. And in the months that follow, the cards are a nice, concrete reminder that the passing of your loved one was noted, and that someone cared, both about the loss associated with that death and the grief that you're experiencing.

There is an unfortunate temptation, however, to get involved in the game of "How many cards/phone calls/flowers were there?" and begin obsessing over these numbers like a collector. If we did not receive (in our estimation) enough expressions of sympathy, does that mean our departed spouses were unworthy of remembrance? Circumstances will differ, social and family circles may be large or small, and many other factors affect the outward displays of support received. The important thing to remember is that every call, every card, and every flower and plant represent a person or family who took the time and trouble to express sorrow for your loss. The volume of the outpouring doesn't make your loss more or less tolerable, nor can it be used to quantify the meaningfulness of the life that has recently come to an end.

Some people periodically go through the cards they received at the time of their initial bereavement, deriving comfort from expressions of support. Others, myself included, find it hard to do so, even after the passage of years. If such a review brings solace, by all means do it. But if you find that the activity continues to be uncomfortable, don't treat the cards as an irreplaceable souvenir. Instead, discard them, just as you would discard a magazine or newspaper from which you've gleaned all the pertinent information. There won't be a quiz later about who delivered a casserole, how many cards were received, or who sent you that potted peace lily.

The most important take-home lesson from all this is that expressions of encouragement are to be received in the spirit of love in which they are offered. But it's wrong to attach significance to the number of cards, flowers, and calls received. And, finally, it's futile and counterproductive, after the death of your spouse, to spend your efforts trying to continually memorialize them. All of us begin to build a memorial of our lives from the time we're old enough to be responsible for our own actions. Let what he or she has built speak for your departed spouse. Cherish the memories of your time together, and begin to go on with your life.

> You yourselves are our letter, written on our hearts, known and read by everyone. (2 Cor. 3:2 NIV)

*Father God, help us to understand that the legacy left behind by our loved ones was built over a period of years. Give us the wisdom to appreciate the eternal parts*

of that heritage, but help us not to dwell on the physical trappings left behind. Give us the courage to be unafraid to look forward, leaning all the while on Your tender mercies. We pray in Your compassionate name, amen.

# Seventeen

# HANDLING THE
# UNFINISHED PROJECTS

The death of a loved one will leave projects and accomplishments undone. Self-imposed pressure to finish what your loved one started may be unrealistic and unhealthy.

*Some friends came by this afternoon and took a bunch of Cynthia's gardening magazines and some of her seedlings. Still some left, and I'll try to find good homes for them this weekend. The remainders go to the nursery next week—they'll be glad to get them. I'm alternately frustrated and depressed by having to deal with so many things that to Cynthia were second nature and to me are a mystery.*

*I had been really "down" about the number of unfinished projects and plans Cynthia left behind—until it dawned on me that, to her, life was a work in progress, and she would have left just as many behind at age ninety-nine as at age sixty-two. And it's foolish of me to think that by completing the projects (which were fun to her, not necessarily to me), I would be honoring her memory. I think she would want me to realize my own limitations, and I can just hear her giggling if I tried to become a gardener. As Allen [our son] said, the worst mistake I could ever make would be to try to live out Cynthia's life for her. So I'll clean up her garden as best I can, put her seedlings up for adoption, tie up the loose ends of her projects, and try to move on. She'd want it that way.* (Author's journal)

It's a significant shock, when walking through the house after the death of your spouse, to encounter projects they will never complete. Whether it's finishing the laundry that overflows the hamper, planting the flowers that sit in rows of pots on the back porch, or knowing what to do with the unfinished painting that sits on the table in the study, dealing with these matters is painful.

There are two primary emotions engendered by unfinished projects. The first is sorrow that your loved one will never again know the feeling of completing an earthly task. Whether it was a household chore or a recreational project, the very presence of the unfinished act reminds us that he or she is gone from this earth for good. Your loved one will never enjoy drinking an early morning cup of coffee, working a crossword puzzle, or digging in the garden. But with this realization should come a companion thought—he or she has not disappeared forever into oblivion. If we, as Christians, truly believe this life is merely a prelude to heaven, our loved one is already in a far better place, experiencing joys that are beyond our comprehension.

Following hard on the heels of grief for our loved one is grief for ourselves. We have been robbed of their companionship, presence, and love. This hurts and will continue to hurt for some time to come. So we try to assuage the pain in a very direct way—by continuing to live their lives for them. The temptation is great to throw ourselves into completing the unfinished tasks in an effort to somehow hang on to our departed loved ones for just a bit longer. Some tasks must, of course, eventually be finished. Clothes must be washed, beds made, and daily household chores carried out. Others can be completed if, and only if, we are up to it. No amount of love, compassion, or aspiration can make a gardener out of someone with an unalterable brown thumb. No excess of desire can turn an untalented dabbler into a painter. In these cases, you may give the projects a good home with someone who shares the interests and talents of the one who left them behind. Some things may be kept, even in an uncompleted state, for sentimental value. And finally, some may be discarded. This is not disrespectful. It merely recognizes that your loved one has moved on. He or she would undoubtedly be the first to tell you, "Don't try to continue living my life for me. Move forward with your own."

As you move on with your life, realize that you too will leave unfinished projects behind. This is a natural outgrowth of living your life to the fullest. We are to continue to live active, productive, and useful lives until we are called to our reward. Projects that are unfinished are a wonderful testament to such a full life.

> How do you know what your life will be like tomorrow? Your life is like the morning fog—it's here a little while, then it's gone. What you ought to say is, "If the Lord wants us to, we will live and do this or that." (James 4:14–15)

～

*Father, we thank You for the lives of loved ones who have gone on to their heavenly reward, leaving behind evidences of an active life here on earth. And we thank You that each day we begin projects we may never finish. Walk with us, direct us, and help us to heal even as we continue to try to resume productive lives, for we know this is the best tribute we can pay to our departed loved ones and to You. In Your name, amen.*

# Eighteen

# REVIEWING THE SOUVENIRS
# OF A LIFETIME

Cleaning out accumulated papers, photos, and souvenirs will often touch off deep emotions. Preparation and attitude adjustment can make this more therapeutic and less traumatic.

*I've been cleaning out papers, clippings, and assorted stuff that Mom had kept. I found magazine articles, newspaper clippings, and gardening tips going back to the time of our marriage! It's not hard to know what to keep and what to toss, but it still stirs up memories and emotions that are sometimes hard to take. I need to do it, but until now I've had to make a schedule so that I only do it for an hour or two each day, and never, ever within a couple of hours of bedtime.*

*This weekend, I decided to bite the bullet and finish the job. I don't think she ever threw out a piece of paper in her life. File drawers and manila envelopes yielded bank statements from banks that don't even exist anymore; Christmas cards and letters; most (if not all) of the birthday, anniversary, valentine, and Mother's Day cards she ever received; ticket stubs and programs from plays we had seen; newspaper clippings about us and you all; and a truckload of other stuff going back for four decades. It wasn't difficult knowing what to keep and what to toss, but while I was doing it, I started crying and just couldn't stop.*

*This morning, in cleaning out some old Sunday school materials* [from when Cynthia was teaching juniors]*, I found a note in her handwriting: "Romans 8:38–39." No explanation, just that Scripture. Talk about a message from beyond the grave—the tears really flowed. But if I truly believe that passage, I can cling to the fact that her death has not separated either of us from God (or from each other except temporarily).* (Author's email to his children)

Each of us accumulates huge amounts of paperwork as we live our lives. Some of it is business material, some represents financial records, and some is purely personal. Very few of us ever get around to going through that mass of paperwork, tossing outdated and unnecessary material, filing what must be kept, and putting personal memorabilia into some kind of order. So, in most instances, it is the survivor—whether a spouse, child, or sibling—who ends up with this task. Be assured that it will trigger some emotions, but that's not all bad.

Going through the papers will undoubtedly take more than one session. Some paperwork must be found quickly, while the passage of time will cushion the emotional blow associated with going through others. In any case, the "keep it or toss it" decision should be made with two factors in mind: the practical and the sentimental. A balance is necessary here. Don't be so practical as to discard material that you'll wish for later, or so sentimental as to discard nothing. If there's a question, put the item aside in a separate pile and consider it at the next cleaning session.

From the practical aspect, begin by keeping bank statements and tax-related documents for three to seven years (check with your accountant). Important documentation that should be identified and kept indefinitely includes papers that prove ownership; legal papers (divorce or property settlements); contracts; and certificates of birth, death, and marriage. The will of the deceased and any pertinent life (and/or accident) insurance policies will be needed. Although you may not feel like doing it, as soon as is practical you will need to begin making a rough draft of the assets owned (individually or jointly) by the deceased at the time of his or her death. This will probably be needed for probate or settlement of the estate.

The decision to keep things for their sentimental value will be affected by individual circumstances. In some families, souvenirs of plays, trips, and special events may have little meaning for anyone other than the couple involved in the activity. Other tangible souvenirs might, however, bring back happy family memories. The question that must be asked repeatedly during this process is "to whom will this be of interest in the future?" If the answer is "no one," the decision to discard becomes easier.

Obviously, photos and videos will be important to future generations and should be kept. The surviving spouse may, however, be the only one able to identify the persons and circumstances in them, which creates an obligation to add explanatory descriptions or captions (on the back of photos, or as labels to videos). Because of the emotions involved, this may be too much for the recently bereaved person to accomplish at this time. Save it for later, and do it in small increments. Future generations will bless the person who takes the time and effort to pass on records that are complete.

The tradition of handing down the family Bible was once common. Nowadays it is unusual to even find such a volume—most homes have several translations, and family members have their own favorite copy. The Bible most often used by a departed loved one, however, may yield something special—favorite passages underlined or annotated, a find that is generally both touching and reveals worshipfulness.

There is never a good time to put one's files in order, but going through papers after the death of a loved one often spurs us to organize our own things, sparing those who come after us some of the difficulties encountered at a difficult time. Doing so is an act of love that may never be acknowledged in our lifetimes, but which will certainly ease the burden of our families in days to come.

But at that time your people—everyone whose name is found written in the book—will be delivered. (Dan. 12:1 niv)

~

*Father, it is difficult to do the mundane tasks left to the living. Help us to hang on to the good memories, to cry healing tears, and to resolve to do what we can to make life easier for those we will someday leave behind. Most of all, may we realize that the most important things we leave in this world cannot be written down or filed, but instead remain forever in the hearts of those we touch for You. In Your eternal and everlasting name, amen.*

*Nineteen*

# Considering a Move

The place that has previously been "home" is no longer the same. Should you consider moving or stay put? It's a hard decision at a time when all decisions are difficult.

*Do I get lonely in this big house by myself? I'd get lonely in a nine by twelve room by myself! There are so many memories here, and I alternate between thinking I don't ever want to leave this place where Cynthia and I lived for the majority of our married life, and wanting to get away from a place where every corner of every room has a memory to remind me that she's gone.*

*Several friends from church have encouraged me to look at the gated community where they live. Since I'm now rattling around in this house alone, it occurs to me that, as a practical matter, maybe I should downsize. But when I looked at three houses on the market in their "enclave," only one was even slightly appealing. And it was about the same size as this one—for about half again as much as this one is worth. So is it worth the financial cost and the considerable effort required to move? Benefit—smaller yard, lots of friends for neighbors. Current status—larger yard, house I'm comfortable in, and lots of friends for neighbors. Decision—stay (at least for now), and get some help with house cleaning and yard maintenance.*

*And this was just one more decision that I wish I could discuss with Cynthia before making it. It's beginning to come home to me—life will never be the same.* (Author's email to his children)

During the weeks when Cynthia was in the ICU, I spent every waking moment at the hospital, rising early to leave the house, and every evening falling into bed exhausted for the bare minimum amount of sleep. As a result, I had no perception that the atmosphere of our house had changed—I was never there. For about a week after her death, my family was with me. Things were certainly different, but I was rarely alone. Then came the time when they returned to their own lives, and I was left to pick up the pieces of mine. That's when I began to notice things were different.

You and your mate may have lived in the same house for decades, or you may have during recent years moved into a smaller dwelling or to a different location. No matter the circumstances, there will be a certain amount of history in the house or apartment you occupied at the time of your spouse's death. These daily reminders of your past experiences may be comforting, as they are to some, or may trigger strong emotions of grief and loss, as they do to many others. Your own situation will be unique, but some common emotions and questions will command your attention.

You'll feel a certain amount of loneliness as you awaken each morning alone and as you contemplate the day ahead. Waves of grief may intrude on your activities as you encounter reminders of past times, and you become freshly aware of your loss. You may find that these triggers are so vivid, and so frequently encountered, that it's difficult to function. Well-meaning friends and family, if they become aware of your emotional roller coaster, will undoubtedly suggest that you make a move at this point. I urge you to consider such a change very carefully before taking any definitive action.

It is never wise to make decisions—especially life-changing decisions—based on acute emotions. An alternate option is to leave your current surroundings temporarily. Take a trip. Yes, you can travel on your own—millions of people do it. Visit friends or relatives. In my own case, dear friends who lived a great distance away were unable to attend the memorial service, so I visited them afterward. The time spent remembering our good times and sharing our grief was therapeutic for them and for me.

If travel is out of the question, change your current surroundings or your routine. Move the furniture around (or have someone else do it, if that's beyond your capabilities). If you have a guest bedroom, sleep there for a while. If you've always had breakfast at the kitchen table, eat in the dining room. If you've routinely taken your morning coffee back to bed and watched the news, take it onto the porch or into the kitchen, and read the paper or have your morning devotions there. Shake things up. There were undoubtedly things that you did as a couple that were more for your spouse than for you—try doing something you like and will enjoy.

On a practical note, any decision to move, whether to a smaller house or apartment or to a different city or state, is a very important one. Experts warn us not to make life-changing decisions for at least a year after the death of a spouse. Unfortunately, this isn't always realistic. Several potentially life-changing decisions are thrust upon us at this time, and some of them can't be put off. In those situations, we should seek advice from family and close friends, as well as contemplate what our spouse would have advised. The decision to move is rarely one that has to be made immediately, and I would urge you to delay it for as long as possible. You may very well find that as the acute shock, grief, and stress abate, the difficulty in concentrating and the mental slowness that plagued you early on will begin to ease, and it will be possible to make decisions more clearly and decisively.

You will, of course, need to pray about these important decisions, remembering that prayer is two-way communication. Don't ask God to bless a decision you have already made. Instead, I urge you to truly seek His will in the matter. Answers don't always come in the form of a burning bush, but quiet time spent in Bible reading and contemplation will never be wasted effort. Remember that wherever life takes you in the future, whether you stay in your current home or move

elsewhere, God will be there with you. Seek His will, as you also seek
His peace.

> I can never escape from your Spirit!
> I can never get away from your presence!
> If I go up to heaven, you are there;
>   if I go down to the grave, you are there.
>                                     (Ps. 139:7–8)

*Eternal Father, guide us in those times when we don't know where to turn or what to do. Give us clarity of thought and decisiveness of purpose, but also give us peace of mind in the decisions we make when we depend on You. May Your Spirit be our comfort and our guide in these days and in all the days of our lives. In Your blessed name, amen.*

# Twenty

# FACING HOSPITAL MEMORIES

For most of us, hospitals trigger painful memories. Visiting the one where your loved one died is especially painful. Here are some recommendations to make such a visit more tolerable.

*I think it's a protective reflex, but I've effectively blocked out of my memory lots of the details of the night Cynthia suffered her stroke. I know that I struggled to convince the local emergency room doctors to transfer her to the University Hospital, where physicians who knew her situation were standing by to do emergency surgery. I know that I spent a sleepless night on a couch in our department chairman's office. I recall alternately sitting in the ICU waiting room reading, and sitting at Cynthia's bedside holding her hand and praying. I remember looking for the slightest sign of improvement and seeing none. And I can never forget sitting down with the neurosurgeon who gave me the news that my medical training had already prepared me to receive—Cynthia was, for all intents and purposes, brain-dead and being kept alive by artificial means. Then came the final nightmare of withdrawing life support, taking care of the after-death details at the hospital, and finally walking out, knowing that I wouldn't be coming back to sit by her bedside anymore. At that point, I truly believed that*

*I could never set foot in an ICU, or even in a hospital, again. I wondered if my days as a practicing physician had come to an end. And I didn't care!* (Author's email to a colleague)

It's impossible for any but the most naive of us to enter a hospital without experiencing emotions. In some instances, that emotion is joy, called forth by the remembrance of the birth of a child; but, in most cases, a hospital visit produces the negative feelings of fear, pain, and grief. After all, hospitals are often "courts of last resort" for the injured, the ill, the dying. And, unless we've been extremely fortunate, by the time we reach middle age, we have in our memory bank one or more recollections of unpleasant experiences within the walls of a hospital.

Death does not come to us exclusively in hospitals; it may find us at home, at work, in vehicles, on vacation, and wherever the human condition exists. But for those whose loved ones spent their last days in a hospital, a return to that particular institution (or any hospital) may be traumatic. Yet we will undoubtedly be called on to make such a visit, and it can't be avoided indefinitely. Is there anything we can do that will help us begin to heal that emotional scar? Fortunately, there is.

First, *go with a purpose.* Your visit should not be about getting back on the horse that threw you, but should be for the purpose of ministering to others. The most likely reason for going will be to visit a friend or relative who is hospitalized, perhaps to sit in a waiting room or at a bedside and comfort a family whose loved one is seriously ill. Resist the temptation to compare their experiences with yours, either in your own mind or (worse yet) in your conversations during the visit. Remember that their sorrow, their worry, their anxiety is fresh while yours is in the past. Focus on your ministry in the moment, and you will be able to put aside your own grief as you do so.

Second, *go with a friend.* If at all possible, make the visit with a close friend or family member. Sharing the experience with another makes it more tolerable. That person will carry half the conversational load, provide a second perspective on events and circumstances, and furnish a listening ear as you ventilate on the drive homeward about your experience.

Finally, *go with God*. You need not do this in your own strength. God has, in fact, promised to be with us in situations that our minds tell us are intolerable. Pray before you go: pray for the one who is ill, for friends and family members who are affected, for the members of the healthcare team who provide care, and certainly for yourself.

As for the physician or nurse reading these pages, let me offer my own personal word of testimony. I did choose to stop practicing in a hospital setting after those two weeks when Cynthia's life hung in the balance in the ICU, but this was part of a planned and staged retirement from medicine. I did return to a part-time office-based practice, although it took almost three months for me to accomplish that. To some degree, the wounds remained raw and painful for a year or more. Even three years later, when I was called upon as a family member to sit once more in a surgery waiting room, and later in an ICU, memories came flooding back. But, as we learn to do early on as healthcare professionals, I was able to put personal feelings aside and function appropriately in the moment. So if you feel that the experience of the loss of your loved one has robbed you of your professional detachment, I can attest that it may, indeed, change your approach and your attitude. But time eventually will prove sufficiently curative for you to resume your healing ministry.

Perhaps you'll be fortunate and never set foot in a hospital after the loss of your loved one. But as our contemporaries age, as modern life presents challenges to health and safety, and as the law of averages eventually catches up to all of us, chances are you'll be called upon to cross that threshold once more. With God's help, you can do it.

> "And when did we ever see you sick or in prison and come to you?" Then the King will say, "I'm telling the solemn truth: Whenever you did one of these things to someone overlooked or ignored, that was me—you did it to me." (Matt. 25:39–40 MSG)

*Father, some things are unpleasant but needful. Help us to look beyond ourselves to the calling You have given each of us to minister to the sick and afflicted. In that ministering, may we continue to find healing ourselves. Through the power of the Great Physician we ask, amen.*

# Twenty-One

# COMBATING FUNERAL FLASHBACKS

Attending a funeral will never be the same after you go through one as chief mourner. Yet your experience provides insight that can be used to minister to others.

*Last week, a wonderful man in our church died. His wife asked that our choir sing for his memorial service. I didn't want to, but I figured it was "payback time" for all that the choir and the church did for me during Cynthia's last illness and at her service. Actually, I could hear one of my "Cynthia tapes" saying, "You really should do this." So I did.*

*The flashback began yesterday when I attended the visitation at the funeral home—the same one that handled Cynthia's arrangements. Today, the order of service had the same picture on the front that was used for Cynthia's. Two of the three ministers at this funeral had also participated in Cynthia's service. And every moment I was in the choir, I pictured myself in that front pew, knowing what those folks were going through, and going through it with them every moment. It was even harder than I had imagined, but I got through it, and felt appropriately self-righteous for making the effort.*

*I came away from the experience with several conclusions. First, there will probably always be an element of "flashback" to your own loved one's memorial service when you attend someone else's. Secondly, there is a tendency to personalize that service in your own image—that is, you place yourself in the position of chief mourner, even comparing yourself to the bereaved one. Third, for a Christian, every funeral should be a celebration of the life of the one who has gone on to be with God, and a time of reassurance that those of us left behind have only been temporarily separated. Finally, if only a person who has suffered the loss of a spouse can truly understand what someone in that situation is going through, then those of us who form that unfortunate "club" should never ignore the opportunity to exercise that ministry.* (Author's journal)

By the time most readers pick up this book, they will have already been through the funeral of a loved one. For the Christian, the funeral serves a number of purposes, some of them common with memorial services of a secular nature. The first function is to allow those left behind to come to grips with the fact that death has truly occurred. The viewing of the deceased, whether in a hospital bed or in a casket, brings a sense of finality to the experience. Families whose loved ones are lost at sea, or otherwise die without a recoverable and identifiable body, are robbed of this, and must work even harder to get to that last stage of grief: acceptance.

A viewing of the deceased may be a catalyst toward acceptance. For years, funerals featured the traditional last viewing, when mourners filed past an open casket, followed by the lid of the casket being closed, signaling the finality of the event. The journey to the cemetery for burial completed the silent testimony that this, indeed, was the end of earthly life for the deceased. But this practice has now been superseded in many instances by one that separates the viewing from the final services.

Instead of open casket viewing at the time of the service, many families are now choosing to receive friends at the funeral home prior to the memorial service. At this visitation, the casket may be open for viewing or may be closed with a picture of the deceased on view. Rather than the public funeral followed immediately by burial, there is often a private commitment service. This service is sometimes limited to family and close friends and is preceded or followed by a more public memorial service with either a secular or a religious theme. In this way, final viewing is separated from the subsequent service, at which the body of the deceased may not even be present.

The substitution of a picture of the departed for a body in the casket during the memorial service may help to accentuate the second function of such a service: honoring the life of the departed. Equally as important, the practice helps to minimize the painful flashbacks family and friends might otherwise experience when they once more enter that building. Memories are linked to many cues, and sitting in the same location where we once experienced such raw grief, looking toward the place where our loved ones' caskets once rested, may bring back more grief, no matter how much time has elapsed.

The third function of a Christian funeral, and the one that sets it apart from secular services, is to emphasize the impermanence of death and the ultimate victory of the Christian over such separation. Many Christian services are referred to as a "celebration of life," and detail not only the positive aspects of the life of the departed but also the ultimate reward of the Christian. This doctrine is important, although most families, caught up in the anguish of the moment, may not be as touched as others attending the service. But, rest assured, in celebrating the life of a Christian there is as much opportunity for an evangelistic occasion as at the most carefully structured and skillfully preached church service.

At some future time, those who have suffered bereavement will be asked to attend a memorial service for a family member or close friend. Frankly, the average person's first reaction is to look for a way out. But generally, attendance can't be avoided, duty wins out over fear, and negative anticipation continues to build. The prospect is not a pleasant one, whether the service is held where your spouse's funeral took place or somewhere different. Upon walking into the church or chapel, the gaze wanders and the mind races to call up memories. Where the casket is sitting is where the body of your spouse or loved one rested. That front pew is where you sat. Perhaps the Scripture passages and prayers have a familiar ring. The emotional responses all this evokes are normal, and no amount of preparation or good advice can prevent them. But it is possible to allow God to work through your reactions in a positive fashion.

Instead of reliving the anguish of your own experience, put yourself in the place of the family who is suffering through this acute loss. Look at the scene through their eyes, with your understanding born of having traveled that road before them. Visualize what you would have liked done for you at this time, and do it for them. You are one of the few persons in that room who fully understands what the bereaved family is going through. You have walked that walk, and, although circumstances may differ, the resulting emotions and responses are remarkably similar.

Quite often, the funeral service is a blur, blotted out from memory virtually as quickly as it takes place. This type of amnesia is a coping mechanism of the mind. But, at a later time, the bereaved often find comfort in listening to the music, the prayers, the Scripture, and the words that were said about their beloved. If the funeral is held in a church, contact someone there and ask if these services are recorded. If a recording of the service is available, purchase a copy, and, after a few weeks, call on the bereaved and offer it to him or her. The bereaved may prefer not to listen to it at that time, and may never do so, but many families appreciate having the option. Recordings could also be shared with those who, for reasons of infirmity or distance, are unable to attend the service. It requires tact and understanding to carry this out, but it is a worthwhile ministry and one from which I personally benefited in my time of grief.

Another small, but often appreciated, gesture is to give the bereaved family one or more copies of the obituary. Extra copies are almost always needed, and this simple, thoughtful gesture can help.

Food is typically brought to the house of mourning in the time immediately following a death. But all of us who have experienced the loss of a spouse or other close loved one know that what we most often need in the weeks after the funeral are evidences of human contact and caring—hugs, phone calls, invitations to dinner. More than this, our experience allows us to truthfully say, "I know how you feel," and to use what we have gone through to help others.

Funerals are a difficult time for those who have suffered a past bereavement, but they are even more traumatic for those whose loss is acute. By placing ourselves in the position of the newly grieving, we Christians can shift the focus of our emotions from reliving trying times to applying the Golden Rule. In this way, God can use even the worst of life's experiences if we allow Him to work through us.

> Why are you looking among the dead for someone who is alive? He isn't here! He has risen from the dead! (Luke 24:5–6)

~

*Father of us all, thank You for Your ability to use the experience of our own bad times to minister to those going through their own deep valleys. Help us to take ourselves out of the picture and to focus on those in need. We know that by doing this, we all will be blessed, and You will be glorified. In Your name, amen.*

# Twenty-Two

# GETTING BETTER—
# FAST OR SLOW?

After the death of a loved one, there sometimes follows a feeling that it would be disrespectful to get over it too soon. There will be plenty of time to experience grief; for quite a while it comes in waves and at the most unexpected times. Don't hesitate to take the good times when they come.

*I hesitate to say it, because I "don't want to get better too soon" (not wanting to be disrespectful to Cynthia's memory, I guess, is the subconscious message), but maybe I'm getting a little better. Hopefully the trend will continue. Still lots of lonely moments, a few tears at the most inopportune and unexplainable times, and I still can't make sense out of any of this. (I guess God can, and someday He can let me in on it.) But I'm managing to get through the day more easily, can see a bit of direction coming back to my life, and even laugh at times. My physician friends have urged me to start on anti-depressants, but I have this feeling that I need to experience the grief, in order to mourn properly.* (Author's email to his children)

*As you know, I was very depressed and emotionally labile during our time together at Christmas, and I sensed that everyone was worried about me. Actually, I was worried about me. So I talked with my internist, and about ten days ago I started on antidepressants. I can't say that there was a sudden, dramatic change, but there definitely has been improvement. I don't have so many of the really down feelings, have less tendency to tear up at the slightest provocation, and sometimes even experience a glimmer of enjoyment of some aspects of life. There's always the faintly perceived guilt that feeling better is somehow disrespectful, but I'm learning to see through that fallacy. I'll always love and miss Cynthia. Feeling better won't change that, but it will make my life more productive.* (Author's later email to his children)

The days and weeks after the loss of a spouse are often spent in crying sprees and bouts of depression, interspersed with activities that have to be done, are performed mainly on automatic pilot, and are largely forgotten afterward. For many of us, the overriding need is twofold: to get through it and to continue to memorialize our lost loved ones and show respect for their memories. The latter emotion often fuels the hurt that we already feel and the continued manifestations of grief. In the twisted logic that pervades these situations, we think that the more we long for our spouses or other loved ones (and the greater degree to which we demonstrate how much we miss them), the more wonderful they were and the better person we are for showing that emotion.

Elisabeth Kübler-Ross, in her book *On Death and Dying* (New York: Macmillan, 1969), listed five stages individuals may be expected to go through when given the news that they are dying. These stages are denial, anger, bargaining, depression, and acceptance. This paradigm was subsequently more widely applied by counselors to individuals receiving news of an impending or present catastrophic loss. Since anyone who has experienced the death of a spouse will agree that the event is certainly catastrophic, it would be expected that progression through these stages is normal and expected. Such is not generally the case, however. For most of us who have walked this road, all these stages are indeed experienced but not necessarily in a neat, orderly, sequential fashion. The person who is grieving may experience two or more of these stages simultaneously, they may come and go in no particular order, ebbing and flowing like ocean waves, and, of them all, depression is the most frequent and persistent.

Is it necessary to experience a certain amount of grief before healing can begin? Probably. Is there a minimum that is necessary, or a maximum beyond which grief becomes pathologic? Not really. Every person's circumstances and psychological makeup are different. It is inadvisable, however, to adopt the stance that "the more grief I experience, the more quickly and completely I'll get over this." Initially, we mourn because our loved ones have experienced the end of life. Even though our Christian faith assures us that they are already in a better place, our humanity wants them to enjoy more of this present world. Greater insight allows us to realize that we are ultimately mourning not their loss of this world's pleasures, but our loss of their companionship—no more time together or experiencing the things we had planned. This level of understanding must be achieved before true adjustment can begin.

The bereaved spouse or the person who has lost a close loved one needs to experience grief to begin the process of getting through it. But there is no benefit to the martyr mind-set (of which I myself was guilty) that refuses the help offered by a professional to prescribe antidepressants. Prayers, counseling, and the support of friends can only go so far for some individuals. The depth of the depression experienced and the total make-up of the individual involved may dictate the need for professional help, and if this involves mood-altering medications prescribed by a professional, I would urge that such a course be followed. One definition of grief is "the normal response to the loss by death of a loved one." Depression following such a catastrophic loss is normal and is referred to by healthcare professionals as "reactive depression." When the depression is excessive or prolonged, however, it becomes pathologic and signals the need for professional help.

At some point—and no one can say exactly when this will be for any one person—it is time to try to move on. Grief counselors sometimes suggest the acronym TEAR to characterize the grief work that is helpful in getting through the grieving process more effectively. It stands for the following:

> **T**o accept the reality of the loss
> **E**xperience the pain
> **A**djust to the new environment
> **R**einvest in reality

Note that this embodies the last of the Kübler-Ross stages—acceptance.

Don't feel that you are abnormal if your experience of grief is what you consider too brief and shallow, or too prolonged and deep. Experience it, but when it takes over your life and keeps you from functioning, seek professional help to allow you to begin to move on. Your loved ones, both the living and the dead, would not want it any other way.

> The LORD is my shepherd,
> I shall not want.
> He makes me lie down in green pastures;
> He leads me beside quiet waters,
> He restores my soul;
> He guides me in the paths of righteousness
> For His name's sake.
> Even though I walk through the valley of the
>     shadow of death,
> I fear no evil, for You are with me.
>
> (Ps. 23:1–4 NASB)

*Father, we ask that You lead us through the valley of the shadow of death, helping us to rejoice for the life of our loved ones, to mourn for our loss, and to look forward with blessed hope and assurance to the day when we shall be reunited with them in Your gracious kingdom. In the name of our Redeemer who makes all this possible, amen.*

# Twenty-Three

# FACING THE HOLIDAYS

The first holidays after the death of a spouse can be gut-wrenching. Christmas is perhaps the hardest holiday of all to get through. Nothing will make things normal, and it's often best to begin as soon as possible to adjust to a new normal.

*Well, I did it! It wasn't easy, but I put up and decorated the Christmas tree. I really thought it would be no problem, because putting up the tree was always my "job." That included getting down all the stuff from the attic, putting up the tree, putting on the lights, putting on the tree skirt, and hanging the colored balls. Cynthia's contribution was walking by the tree several times a day, pulling an ornament out of the box, and putting it on the tree.*

*No one loved to celebrate Christmas more than Cynthia, and I just couldn't not put up the tree. I got it up, strung the lights, and got most of the ornaments on without too much of a problem. But when it came time to put the angel on the top of the tree with the angel ball marked "Mom" just below it, I sort of lost it. But the finished product looks good, and I think she would approve. I guess every day is Christmas in heaven, but knowing Cynthia, she's sneaking a peek to see that we do it right at our house also. (Author's email to his children)*

After the death of a spouse, or of any loved one, the year that follows is filled with holidays and special dates that will trigger strong emotions and memories: birthdays, wedding anniversary, Christmas, New Year's. The first time each of these occurs is always the hardest to deal with, and it's important to prepare emotionally for this year of firsts. That first Christmas will be, hands down, the most difficult holiday to face.

Every family has traditions, and the strongest of these are those practices associated with the holidays. Cynthia and I always put up the Christmas tree a couple of weeks early, topping it every year with the same cardboard and cloth angel she and I placed atop our very first tree. When I realized it would be up to me to both put up the tree (my usual job) and to decorate it (Cynthia's self-appointed task), I cried. That example is symbolic of the problems encountered in getting through that first Christmas without your spouse.

If your mate dies in the fall or winter, Christmas seems to come almost immediately, and you'll undoubtedly be unprepared. You'll, in fact, be unprepared for that first Christmas no matter how long you have to get ready. Your shopping may have been completed earlier, but you're unable to discover where your husband or wife stowed some of the presents. If you haven't shopped, you'll find it a Herculean task to decide on and purchase presents. Christmas cards present a special challenge, because some of the folks on your list won't have heard about your loss. This will call for notes of explanation, notes that seem to open up fresh wounds with each one you write.

If you are a widower left with the daunting task of providing Christmas dinner for the family, you will likely feel totally helpless. For me, taking over the simple everyday cooking chores was disastrous. On the other hand, seeing other family members in the kitchen, preparing the meal your wife would have made, may bring floods of tears and place you, as it did me, in the depths of despair. And the problem is just as gut-wrenching for the new widow trying to carry on as though nothing has changed.

One of the strongest urges for those who celebrate their first Christmas after the death of a spouse is to keep everything as normal as possible. This urge is understandable, but it's also ill-advised. Many of us don't recognize our mistake, however, until after we experience the unfortunate consequences of those attempts. Everything that takes place, from the opening of presents to the family meal, presents a strong reminder of the loss you and your family have suffered. It's advisable at this first Christmas to consider establishing new traditions, new ways of doing things, and a new normal.

If possible, the family meal should be at a different location, perhaps at the home of one of the children. The exchange of gifts should be simplified to relieve everyone, as much as possible, from the pressure of choosing and purchasing presents. Focus on the younger generations, wherever possible. Delight in the joy that children always bring to Christmas. Include attendance at a church service if you can, and make the time together one of family sharing. Avoid emphasis on "getting it right." It won't be right, in any conventional sense, because of the conspicuous absence of the departed loved one. Accept this, be prepared for tears and unexpected emotional tides, and support one another. Remember that others will be feeling the same grief and loss that is affecting you.

There will undoubtedly be some sense of depression at celebrating Christmas in this different fashion. The feeling is not abnormal, and, in fact, is a normal phenomenon called "reactive depression." Its effects can be lessened, however, by appropriate medical pretreatment. If you've been avoiding contacting your physician to discuss taking an antidepressant, you'd be well-advised to do so at least a month before Christmas, since most of these medications require two weeks or more of regular administration to reach maximum effect. And it's important to remember that alcohol accentuates, rather than relieves, depression.

Although holiday depression is common (while self-limited), there is no truth to the long-held belief that there are more suicides during the Christmas holidays than at other times. If, however, you do find yourself thinking, "I can't live like this," or "I can't go on," immediately talk with a family member, friend, pastor, or counselor.

The first Christmas is the hardest. They get easier with the passage of time. Let yourself experience the grief, but don't feel you're being disrespectful if you find yourself laughing at times. Remember that the One whose birth we celebrate on this date later died, but His glorious resurrection has given hope to all of us, especially to those whose loved ones have gone on to the reward that He purchased.

> For everything there is a season,
>      a time for every activity under heaven.
> A time to be born and a time to die.
>      A time to plant and a time to harvest. . . .
> A time to cry and a time to laugh.
>      A time to grieve and a time to dance.
>                                   (Eccl. 3:1–2, 4)

∿

*Father, when we celebrate the birth of Your Son, it's an emotional time, one that reminds us of our own mortality, while bringing to mind the eternal life that awaits us when this life is completed. We thank You for the time we had with our loved ones who have gone on to enjoy that life with You, and we pray that in the midst of our grief You will give us the gift of acceptance and grace, that we may complete our time here in a way that will please and glorify You. In the name of Your Son, amen.*

# Twenty-Four

# REMEMBERING AN
# ANNIVERSARY

All of us dread the first anniversary of the loss of our loved one. As one friend put it, "There are some anniversaries you shouldn't keep celebrating."

*Today is the first anniversary of Cynthia's death. I was able to arrange for a Coast Guard craft to take me to the spot off the Texas coast where I scattered her ashes almost a year ago. I planned to read a Scripture, pray, and toss a single red rose on the water. I was so anxious for everything to be perfect. I stopped at a flower shop on the drive to South Padre Island and found the rose I wanted. All during the drive down I rehearsed what I was going to say. I put the rose in the hotel minibar to keep it fresh. I set my alarm and left a wake-up call.*

*I couldn't eat breakfast—just coffee. I got to the Coast Guard station half an hour early. The seaman in charge of the detail apologized that a relatively small boat was the only one available, since all the others were out of service for repair. We were just approaching the spot for the memorial when he received an urgent radio message to "abort the mission and respond immediately—report of a fire on a vessel." The twin 240 hp engines almost lifted the craft out of the water as he raced back to the Coast Guard station for equipment and additional crew, while I tossed the rose overboard, said a silent prayer, and hung on for dear life.*

*I found myself thinking that somewhere Cynthia must be laughing about all this. I think it was fitting that this carefully planned memorial, which was so important to me, turned into a real "fire drill." It didn't matter so much what was or was not said when I threw that rose into the water—the most significant thing is that I took the time to think about it, to reflect on what has transpired over the past twelve months, and to ask God to grant me strength and guidance in moving forward with my life. I think that's the important stuff, and it wasn't lost in the urgency of the moment as we sped over the water of the Gulf of Mexico. Cynthia, you are remembered, loved, and very much missed. And no one could have enjoyed the farce that played out today more than you.* (Author's journal)

No one ever forgets the date of his or her spouse's death. It provokes an emotion unmatched by prior experience. The initial shock of a death often provides some emotional insulation, as we move on autopilot through the first few weeks afterward. As reality sets in, however, we may note that we cry without apparent provocation, feel depressed with no evident cause, and suffer emotional lability that mimics a roller-coaster ride. Each time we're reminded of our loved one's death, especially during this first year, it will present a severe challenge.

For the first several months after Cynthia's death, I became more depressed on the fourteenth of every month (the day she suffered her stroke) and the twenty-eighth of every month (the day she died). It reached the point that for two or three days before these two dates I began dreading them, until finally about half my month was spent in dreading, experiencing, or recovering from the anniversary of those dates. In addition, I found myself wanting to commemorate the occasion in some fashion—doing something that would keep

Cynthia's memory fresh in my mind and remind myself and others of how wonderful she was and how she is missed. Grief saps both physical and mental energy, and makes it extremely difficult to accomplish anything worthwhile. Adding in this preoccupation for proper "celebration" of these dates essentially halved my already diminished productivity. Others who have suffered the death of a spouse may undoubtedly be similarly challenged.

Although it's not abnormal to ascribe importance to the day of the month when you suffered your loss, I would encourage you to try to work through as quickly as possible the need to do so. Try to be with friends or family on the first few of these monthly anniversaries. Occupy yourself with productive activities, and stay busy, with one notable exception. At a time of your choosing, pause to take a few quiet moments to reflect on the good times you had with your spouse, to thank God for those blessings, and to quietly pray for support and direction for your future. Set aside this time to purposefully commemorate the day, and then try to move on and not look back. The next such event will come soon enough. And soon a year will have passed.

The first anniversary of the death is a watershed in the grieving process. You have completed your year of firsts—the first Christmas, New Year's, wedding anniversary, birthday—and everything you hear and read tells you that things should be easier from here on. My first advice is not to have unrealistic expectations in this regard. From my own experience, the passage of years does indeed dull the influx of emotions that mark the anniversary of the death of your spouse, but even after several years that date will continue to trigger emotions that will cause you to stop and reflect. So set aside a specific time of meditation and prayer, and allow yourself to mark the occasion. Then try to be busy and productive for the balance of the day. Spend time with family or friends if that's possible. If not, find an activity that has a redemptive purpose: visit a shut-in, volunteer to deliver Meals on Wheels, arrange to help in an after-school program. Do something outward directed, to avoid focusing on yourself.

The second bit of advice is to focus future commemorative efforts not so much on the day of your spouse's death as on his or her birthday. Do something in your spouse's name—altar flowers at church, a memorial donation to a worthy charity, an unselfish act of kindness—and mark the day on which your spouse entered the world, rather than when he or she left it. Although the first birthday after your spouse's death may be one of those anniversaries you'll have trouble getting through, you'll find it more easily becomes a time of rejoicing because of his or her life, rather than depression because of his or her death.

Nothing that reminds you of your loss will be easy to take. With God's help, and the support of friends and family, each passing year will make the occasion easier to mark. The times of sadness occasioned by your loss may never go away completely, but the frequency and severity of the reaction will diminish. Healing in the true sense probably never occurs, but the wound does eventually close, leaving only a tender scar.

> Should I mourn and fast in the fifth month, as I have done for so many years? (Zech. 7:3 NIV)

> A good and honest life is a blessed memorial. (Prov. 10:7 MSG)

*Father of the ages, to whom eternity is but a moment, we thank You for the time we were given with our dearly loved ones. Help us to realize that they are even now in Your presence. Help us to celebrate their lives, and give us the direction, strength, and encouragement to get on with ours. In Your blessed name, amen.*

# Twenty-Five

# BEING OPEN TO A SECOND CHANCE

"I'll never love anyone again the way I loved my spouse." This is the characteristic reaction of the person whose spouse has died. But as time softens the impact of the grief, it is wise to be open to the possibility that God may have prepared another companion with whom to share your life.

*It's been more than nine months since Cynthia passed away. Three months after I met her, we were "going steady" (my daughter assures me that no one uses that term anymore), and after six months we were engaged, although marriage had to wait for her graduation from nursing school. We were virtually inseparable for the forty-three years we had together, forty as husband and wife. I have mourned and continue to mourn her death. But, as she would have been the first to remind me, life goes on and there is no reason to sit here crying for the rest of my life.*

*About three months ago, I finally decided that I could no longer tolerate subsisting on frozen dinners eaten in silent meditation in front of the TV, and got up my nerve to ask someone to go to dinner with me, just to talk. Kay started out as my secretary almost twenty-six years ago. Now she has a responsible managerial position at the medical school. Cynthia and I have known her two sons from their childhood, and she in turn is well-known to my children. She has been alone for fifteen years, and I felt that she knew me and could relate to my loss better than almost anyone. We've enjoyed talking, she's been understanding and supportive, and we've begun to go out to dinner on a fairly regular basis. I don't know where this will lead, but I guess right now this could be considered "dating." I've agonized over this, and decided that Cynthia wouldn't feel I was dishonoring her memory by dating at this point. Rather, my friends have assured me that this is a testament to the joy and fulfillment I found in our marriage, leading me to seek companionship because of the good life Cynthia and I had. I'll never find another Cynthia, nor do I even try. But I have found someone who makes me laugh again and has given me a reason to look forward to each new day, an emotion that I thought I would never again experience.* (Author's email to friends)

Among the array of emotions felt by a grieving widow or widower, foremost is a certain kind of sadness—a sadness engendered by the knowledge that the spouse whom the bereaved loved for so many years, the spouse who loved that widowed person so intimately and knew him or her so well, has passed from this present life. The widowed person's own life has changed in so many ways, one of which is the absence of this other person who completed his or her life.

There can be two reactions to this situation: bereaved persons can bury themselves in self-pity and sorrow, or they can make an attempt to rebuild their lives—restructuring it to be more independent, reaching out to establish support systems, and broadening their horizons. The first path is one that obviously leads in a vicious circle, a downward spiral of turning inward, eventually ending in depression and a life without meaning or fulfillment. The other, more difficult, course of action will not be easy, nor will progress be rapid or even steady. The time of acute grief saps our energy, takes away our initiative, and fosters inaction. It is necessary to experience all that to whatever degree is needed, but even during these dark days the newly single person must begin to look outward and forward.

Some of the things that go into constructing a new life can include outwardly directed actions such as an increased involvement in your church, participation in a social club, and activities such as golf and tennis. Some solitary activities may also help fill the empty hours: painting, reading, writing, needlework, just to name a few. Each individual must find those things that hold his or her interest and occupy his or her time fruitfully. First, though, that person must be open to the concept and make an effort to begin.

There is one other eventuality with which the person who has suffered the death of a spouse must contend. After experiencing such a loss, it is natural to think, "I have loved, and my loved one is now dead. I can never love again." This may well be true, and many people live a happy and productive life after being widowed, never remarrying or establishing a new romantic relationship. My experience has placed me in contact with many persons, both men and women, who have formed fruitful single lives for themselves after the death of their spouses. Although generalizations are dangerous, it certainly seems that women adapt to the newly single life much better than do men.

There remains the possibility, nevertheless, that God has prepared someone to share your future life. I would encourage you to be open to that possibility. None of us are ready to date right after the loss of our mates, and the period of time before we can even consider that prospect will be highly variable: certainly a matter of many months, perhaps years. But loneliness may eventually lead you to seek opportunities for conversation or companionship. These relationships may remain purely platonic, but you may be surprised to find them blossoming into—could it be?—love.

Our culture has led us to believe that for every man or woman, there is one perfect mate. When that match is dissolved by death, we've been conditioned to think that there'll never ever be another love in our lives. I don't begin to understand how this can be, but I can attest that it's possible for God to place in our paths other individuals whom we can love and cherish. The circumstances that bring two such persons together temper and condition the love they develop. A second love late in life can blossom and mature more quickly, because older people have life experiences that educate them to the realities of love. Young people in love have what seems like an endless life span ahead of them; while those of us in the autumn of our lives realize full well the finite number of years available to us, and we're hesitant to waste any of that valuable time.

Any such relationship is subject, of course, to survivor guilt and a sense of being unfaithful to the departed spouse. It's necessary to first of all ask yourself whether your husband or wife would want you to be happy. The answer is undoubtedly yes. Secondly, you should re-examine your wedding vows. They almost certainly included some variation of the phrase "until death parts us." After losing your spouse, it's typical to put thoughts of a new relationship out of your mind, and to hang on with all your might to any vestige of your lost relationship. Now it's time to realize that the bonds of marriage have been broken, not through any act of our own will or volition but against our wishes. If a new relationship seems to be forming, it's necessary to consider the preceding stipulations and to form a new mind-set.

Whether you remain single for the rest of your life or God prepares you for another union, your first marriage cannot and should not be ignored or buried in your memory. Recognize how it influenced and shaped your life. You may, and you should, continue to love your first husband or wife. It's possible to do that and at the same time commit yourself to another marriage. And commit is exactly what you must do, should you be so blessed. Don't make a habit of comparing your new spouse with your first one, your new circumstances with your previous ones. Constantly endeavor to give the person you are marrying your full measure of love and devotion. Admittedly, it's a balancing act to move forward with your new husband or wife while honoring your first one. But it's possible, and like most good things in life, well worth the effort.

Finally, before taking the final step into matrimony, you should talk frankly with your potential new spouse, and make sure that he or she understands the possible pitfalls and your commitment to avoid them. If he or she understands, and you both feel true mutual love, then you both are truly blessed.

Whatever the future holds for you, remember that God is with you in this journey. He was beside you in the dark days surrounding the death of your husband or wife. He remains an ever-present source of comfort and guidance. And He offers each of us, those now living and those who have passed from this world, the blessed prospect of eternal life through Him. My prayer is that He will continue to guide you in the days to come.

> "For I know the plans I have for you," says the LORD. "They are plans for good and not for disaster, to give you a future and a hope." (Jer. 29:11)

~

*Our most kind and gracious Father, watch over those who suffer and grieve. Supply comfort and encouragement, give grace for each moment, and lead us through the valley of the shadow of death into the bright light of Your eternal kingdom. Help us to keep our eyes and our lives focused on You. In the end, draw us to You. In the name of our Savior, Jesus, we pray, amen.*

# Twenty-Six

# TELLING YOU MY BACKSTORY

For those who would like to know the story behind the main story, here are the details of my own loss.

*On September 14, 1999, Cynthia drove herself the four blocks to the athletic club. She was recovering from surgery for a fractured ankle suffered the month before, and had gone to do some upper body stretches. They called me about an hour later to tell me that she had suddenly lost consciousness while starting her workout. The paramedics and I arrived at about the same time.*

*Because she had suffered a transient stroke in April 1998, she had undergone an arteriogram, which showed an abnormal collection of blood vessels at the base of the brain. This presented the potential to rupture without warning. The choice came down to living fully, and probably dying suddenly if a rupture occurred, as opposed to surgery, which carried the risk of a neurologic deficit, major or minor. She took extensive counsel with our skilled neurosurgeons, and, after weighing everything, she chose not to have elective surgery. We talked long and hard about this choice, and it was her decision—I'm not sure I could have changed her mind, and I certainly didn't try.*

*When I got to her, Cynthia had obviously suffered a massive stroke, and I was sure the blood vessels in the brain had ruptured. We stabilized her at the local hospital (which is an excellent facility), and then helicoptered her to the university hospital at the medical center where I am on the faculty. She went immediately from the helipad to radiology for a CAT scan, then to surgery for an emergency procedure to reduce pressure and stop the bleeding—all this in less than four hours from the time of the acute episode.*

*Following this surgery, which dealt with the acute problem and removed the vascular mass, she never came out of what was essentially the deepest level of coma. The operating neurosurgeon felt, he told me later, that by a minute or so after the acute bleeding episode, she had suffered irreversible brain damage. After two weeks, it was obvious that she was functioning only on upper spinal cord reflexes and a minute amount of the brain stem. It was also obvious that there was absolutely no chance she would ever be a sentient human being again, even if kept alive on life support for a prolonged period. Cynthia and I had long ago executed living wills and had discussed this scenario many times, and on September 28 I did the hardest thing I have ever done in my life—I agreed with the neurosurgeon to discontinue life support. An hour later, Cynthia passed away quietly.*

*Tissue donation was carried out in accordance with her expressed wishes, and was followed by cremation. We held a memorial service for her on September 30 at our church. With the assistance of the Coast Guard, I carried out a burial at sea by scattering her ashes off the coast of South Padre Island, where we had so many wonderful times.*

*My friends and colleagues, both here and around the world, were very supportive through the two weeks of hell on earth I experienced while she was in the ICU and after her death. Hundreds of memorial gifts were made in her memory—to our church and to our professional societies (both hers and mine). It's obvious that Cynthia touched many lives, and I think she would be both pleased and a bit surprised at this outpouring, since she was such a quiet, humble person.*

*Before her memorial service, one of our friends said Cynthia was "an angel in a girl suit." And our pastor ended his eulogy by saying, "There aren't enough Cynthia Mabrys in the world." Amen to that.* (Author's email to a number of friends throughout the country, informing them of Cynthia's death)

If I were to choose a Scripture to characterize Cynthia's life, I could never find a better one than that read by one of our former pastors at her memorial service:

An excellent woman [one who is spiritual, capable, intelligent, and virtuous], who is he who can find her? Her value is far more precious than jewels and her worth is far above rubies or pearls. (Prov. 31:10 AMP)

*Father, we give You thanks for all the saints who have gone before us, and whose lives have reflected You far better than any sermons or prayers that we might offer. May we too be an example for those who come after us. In Your name, amen.*

*Twenty-Seven*

# MARRIED . . . AGAIN

I know of no surviving spouse who immediately thinks of remarrying. The grief is too raw. The emotions still say, "I'll never love another the way I loved my spouse." And that's true. But for some of us God has prepared another mate to help assuage the loneliness we feel. True, survivor guilt could prevent us from even considering such a thing for a while, perhaps indefinitely. The time frame varies with the person and situation, but eventually a number of bereaved spouses will get past that and find themselves thinking of marrying again.

Statistics tell us that women are less likely than men to remarry after the death of their spouse, but statistics can't be translated into individual situations. Both men and women may face the question of being open to another mate. They may elect to remain single or may remarry. There's nothing wrong with choosing the former course. This chapter, though, is for those who choose to marry again.

Some men need a wife to "complete" them, not just to cook and clean. Most of us have found somewhere along the way that we can do that—even folding fitted sheets when necessary. I believe that what men and women alike really look for when they remarry is a companion, someone with whom they can share their remaining life.

Should a surviving spouse even consider remarriage? The Bible is silent, or at least not directive, on the specifics of this question. Paul both encourages and discourages the practice (1 Cor. 7:8–9; 1 Tim. 5:14), in effect leaving it to the individual involved. Jesus, when asked a question about who would be a woman's husband in Heaven after she was married multiple times, told the religious leaders who asked the question that marriage as we know it doesn't exist in the afterlife (Luke 20:33–35). In other words, the afterlife shouldn't be a consideration in the question of remarrying here on earth.

That having been said, what follows are some things I have discovered after I accepted the gift God had prepared for me in Kay. A second marriage can be a wonderful thing, and I've heard it said repeatedly that the very act of remarrying is a testament to the success of the first marriage. The marriage to the deceased spouse may have been so good that one looks forward hopefully to another. Of course, that may not always be true. Perhaps the first marriage wasn't ideal. If that's so, this is an opportunity to try for a better result. In either case, there are differences between a first and second marriage that we would do well to keep in mind.

Let me say up front that these observations and suggestions are based on my own experience and that of some of my peers. They're primarily applicable to older individuals who have lost their spouse and subsequently remarried. They deal with a blended family, which is what most of us enter into with a second marriage. And they are offered here to show that there is hope for those who marry again.

> "For I know the plans I have for you," says the LORD. "They are plans for good and not for disaster, to give you a future and a hope." (Jer. 29:11)

*You're both more mature.* One thing you have going for you in this process is the maturity developed through years of experience in dealing with challenges. The number of years remaining in this marriage may be shorter than with your first, but they can be just as sweet, so long as you realize that you can't simply sit back and depend on what you did before. New situations will develop each day, and your maturity will be an asset in handling them.

It's likely that you and your deceased spouse made adjustments throughout your marriage, and these took place over a long period of time. With a second marriage, it will be necessary for you to do the same thing again. If you're as impatient as I am, you might like for them to be immediate, but the changes won't happen overnight, nor will the situations for compromise all make themselves known in the first few months or even years of your marriage. Kay and I had developed some pretty firmly fixed ways of doing things, and they were not the same, so we needed to deal with that difference. Adjustment and compromise were necessary. Those are words you'll read several times in this chapter—and there's a reason for it.

You and your second husband or wife will probably have some differences in lifestyle and preferences. You may be a morning person and your new spouse may not get going until noon. He or she might have different tastes than you in food . . . or TV programs . . . or the kind of car to drive. To solve these differences as they manifest themselves, changes will be necessary. Be careful, though, that one individual doesn't make all the adjustments in these situations.

*There will be disagreements.* You might have considered your first marriage to be ideal. You and your husband or wife never disagreed—or, at least, that's what you remember. The truth is that the passage of time tends to erase the bad times and accentuate the good. That's as it should be, but it's wise to realize that much of what you recall as good in your prior marriage was the result of honing the rough edges and smoothing corners over a period of years. These didn't just happen. They were the result of accommodations made by both you and your spouse.

Now you're going to go through the same process again, and there will be disagreements. These may be over major problems or minor situations, but they'll require expression of opinions before you reach an eventual compromise. Just because you'd answered these questions in your previous marriage doesn't mean they won't come up in this new one. They will. It's normal, and chances are you'll get through them with your new marriage not only intact but stronger than ever.

I was surprised when Kay and I first disagreed. I suppose I figured that this marriage would be perfect from the start. After all, we'd both been married before. We should have worked these things out. Then I realized that this, too, was part of the adjustment process. We eventually discovered how to handle our disagreements, and I trust you will too. They're a normal part of any marriage, whether first or second.

*You'll be different because of your loss.* My outlook and parts of my personality changed with the death of my first wife, and some of those changes linger to this day. For instance, after Cynthia's death I became much more tender. I found myself crying openly after certain songs and hymns. Fifteen years later, I still do this at very unexpected times. After her passing, I made a vow to consider every day a gift from God. I try to keep that in mind on a daily basis. I don't always succeed, but I try. There was definitely a change in my attitude after her death.

The changes Kay experienced were different from mine, but no less real. It took me a long time to discover some of these, and more crop up from time to time. But knowing they are there and being ready to deal with them gives me a leg up on responding.

Your mutual understanding of each other's quirks and foibles can't be hurried. Just because you might have known each other for a long time doesn't mean that you'll immediately adjust to one another. Kay and I might have thought we knew about each other, but that was in a work setting. There was a lot more for both of us to learn. It was a matter of years before we developed the needed sense of familiarity in a personal setting. And it's an ongoing process.

*You're not just marrying one person.* When you marry for the first time, you may not give as much thought as you should to the way your in-laws will fit into your life. Whether your relationship with them is distant or close, eventually you settle into a routine. You may see them from time to time, but mostly it will be just you and your spouse, plus whatever children God adds to your family. That's the family unit you're used to, but it changes after the death of your wife or husband. And there's an even greater change when you remarry.

When you marry for a second time, the parents of your bride or groom may be dead, or divorced, or separated from you by distance. But there are a number of others who also form a part of your new family. There will be siblings of your spouse to meet and interact with. Some you'll see regularly because they live nearby. With others, your major contact will be by phone or the Internet. And just as you will need to accept this part of your new husband's or wife's family, your spouse needs to do the same. Each of you will help the other in this endeavor.

Probably most important of all, children and even grandchildren will be added to the family you've grown accustomed to. There will be names to learn, details to absorb, and schedules to dovetail with yours. Despite the juggling necessary to accomplish all this, there are positives from this addition.

The natural inclination of some individuals who remarry is to separate the branches of the family into "mine" and "yours." This may be natural, but in the long run it isn't healthy. There will undoubtedly be a period of adjustment, and one of the things you'll need to overcome is the natural tendency to favor your family, especially the children and grandchildren, over any from the other side of the marriage. This may be the stickiest situation you'll encounter.

The true blended family is just that—family gatherings come to include all the siblings, children, and grandchildren from both sides. Sometimes it isn't possible because of geographic separation. In other situations, true blending never takes place because of attitudes or expectations. But it's always necessary to strive for the ideal if at all possible. Eventually, you and your spouse will find what works in your case. And don't be discouraged if your result isn't what you envisioned or want. Every marriage—even a second marriage—is different.

*Your new spouse is a different person.* Kay had worked with both Cynthia and me for many years. She recognized and respected our relationship. However, early in our marriage she had to point out to me that she wasn't Cynthia. Her habits, her behaviors, her desires were different. When she called that to my attention, it made me realize that there were times when I fell back into habits I had formed during my first marriage. Of course, the reverse can be true, and sometimes Kay was influenced by events that took place before she and I became husband and wife.

We didn't forget what had gone before. Instead, we recognized that we had formed a new union. Although the lessons we each learned in our prior marriages were important, what we do in the future will be unique to us.

One of the things I sometimes hear from individuals who have remarried is that they occasionally dream about their first spouse. There is nothing abnormal about this, and it shouldn't produce guilt. Likewise, in almost every case of a second marriage there will come a time when you call your new husband or wife by the name of the first one. Such a slip isn't the end of the world.

A good friend who remarried after the death of his first wife told me of the time he referred to his new wife by the wrong name. She simply smiled and said, "Think nothing of it . . ." then appended the name of her deceased husband. She understood that an error like this was normal.

I still recall that there were times in this second marriage when I sometimes flashed back to memories of my time with Cynthia. These private memories are normal, and generally become less frequent with time. A more difficult situation occurred when I had trouble remembering with which wife I made such-and-such a trip. I have found that the only way to handle this is truthfully, and on more than one occasion I asked Kay if she recalled a situation or a journey, only to have her gently remind me that I must have done that with Cynthia.

The situations of using the wrong name or wondering which wife was involved became fewer and fewer for Kay and me the longer we lived together. Early in our marriage, after I apologized for such a lapse, Kay reminded me that it wouldn't be long before we made memories of our own. And she was right. Soon I no longer worried about recalling my old memories. I was making new ones.

One of the worst mistakes either you or your new husband or wife can make is to try to remake the other in the image of the deceased spouse. Just because your previous mate did or said a particular thing doesn't mean that your new spouse will react in the same way. Whether consciously or unconsciously, you may ascribe actions or feelings to the person you're marrying that are a carryover from your first marriage. If you find yourself in this situation, take a moment to think about what you're doing and the reason you're reacting this way. Recalibrate your feelings. This may be a natural tendency, but it's one that you'll need to get past to make the second marriage successful.

Chances are that your initial marriage ceremony included a promise to love, cherish, honor, and be faithful to your new bride or groom. You didn't specifically promise to always consider the effect on your spouse of your actions, but it didn't take long for you to start doing just that. Soon you made most decisions with both you and your spouse in mind. Even after death dissolved that union, some of these priorities remained. For instance, shortly after Cynthia's death, when I contemplated a trip I automatically thought of whether she'd like to go. It took a while for me to adjust to her absence. After my second marriage, I began to consider not only Kay but also certain members of our extended family who were not in the equation before.

In-laws, children, actions, names—getting used to the new situation will require time and effort on the parts of you and your new wife or husband. You're starting over, and the adjustment won't be quick or easy. So long as both of you are willing to make that adjustment with love, the end result will be a strong union that will last for however many years of life God grants you.

*Your horizons will be broader.* After the death of a husband or wife, many people retreat into their shells. Remarrying brings them out, sometimes willingly but occasionally grudgingly. I found in the time after Cynthia's death that all activities, from eating out to attending a social gathering, were much more difficult for the single individual than for a couple. Marrying for a second time changes this.

A friend whose first wife was something of an introvert married a woman with the personality, the circle of friends, and the social calendar of an extrovert. He found himself delivering Meals on Wheels, attending different church functions, and meeting a whole new group of her friends and acquaintances. Like it or not, he was thrust into this new situation, and he quickly adapted to it. His horizons were expanded.

I'm not saying that every remarriage will thrust the widow or widower into an abundance of new activities. What I can say with assurance is that the second marriage will make it more difficult for the individual to sit in a darkened room and withdraw. Whether it is a little or a lot, one can expect a change in lifestyle with a second marriage. Take advantage of it.

*A final word.* Have the past fifteen years together been without a flaw for Kay and me? Not at all. Have there been adjustments and compromises? Certainly. But am I glad I entered again into the state of matrimony? Definitely. Do I think Cynthia would approve? I think the answer to that question is a definite yes. Your journey will be different from mine, but with God's direction, I trust it will be a good one.

Let me close with what I said before the small group of family and friends who assembled for my own second wedding. I'll admit that I haven't always lived up to these vows, but I've tried. I hope they're meaningful to you.

*To my family: For forty years I was privileged to share a marriage with a wonderful woman who was my wife and your mother. You saw that relationship, and I hope that it is a template that you will use in your own lives. During those forty years, Cynthia and I talked about literally everything, and many times we discussed the role of the surviving spouse, although usually with the expectation on my part that it would be her who was left behind. I feel very certain, based on those conversations and our relationship, that Cynthia would give her approval to my entering into marriage with Kay. But in the same breath, I need to assure each of you that this new relationship does not, and cannot, detract from the love I held and hold for Cynthia, nor can or will it diminish the love I hold for each of you. This does not signal the demise or diminution of that feeling, but simply expands the dimensions of our family, now including a wonderful woman who I can assure you loves and cares for each of you deeply. I want to thank you for your love for me during the past year and a half, love which has firmly undergirded me at a time when I truly felt that other than you I had nothing for which to live. Kay has not replaced my feelings for you, but instead shares them. In summary, I loved and will always love Cynthia, and that love, as well as my love for each of you, is not diminished by what we do today.*

*To Kay's family: Kay and I have known each other for over a quarter of a century. Working side by side, you can get to know the worst, as well as the best, of anyone, and over the years we developed a mutual trust and respect. Until a year ago, we never thought of ourselves in any relationship other than that dictated by our work. But over the past year, as we have developed an entirely different perspective, we have been pleased (but not surprised) to find that the persons we had come to know in the office were not merely public personas, donned like a mask to hide private imperfections. We've discovered that not only do we like each other, we have come to love each other. We've carefully and prayerfully looked at the circumstances that brought us together, and both have concluded that our relationship is not based on a feeling of rebound and need, but rather represents a gift from a loving God, who never causes bad things to happen, but who can bring good out of them for those who love Him and trust in Him. To Kay's sons, I cannot and do not wish to replace your father, but do wish you to know that I care for each of you as though you were my own. I promise you that I will continue to love and cherish Kay, and that each of you will never find your place in her heart diminished because I am also in that heart.*

*To Kay: A year and a half ago, I despaired of ever having any joy in my life. A year ago a kind and merciful God influenced me to seek the counsel and company of someone I'd known for many years, who had also suffered a traumatic loss in her life, and whom I hoped could be a sounding board for the emotions I was experiencing. We both were unprepared for the deepening relationship that seemed to develop so effortlessly and rapidly from that innocent beginning. And finally, we accepted it for what it was and is—a gift from God. You have been wonderfully sensitive and caring as I navigated the stormy waters of grief and loss, and have been open in your support and in encouraging me never to forget what I had with Cynthia. In years past, I learned to respect you and admire your many wonderful qualities. In the past year, I have come to love you. What we will build together, starting today, will be ours, and I have no doubt that it will be very special for both of us. I thank you for making my life complete again, and I pledge to you my love, for as long as God allows us life.*

*Ecclesiastes 4 says: "Two are better than one . . . for if either of them falls, the one will lift up his companion. But woe to the one who falls when there is not another to lift him up" (NASB). And to that, I can only say, "Amen."*